MODEL
RAILWAYS
AND THEIR BUILDERS
BY
JACK RAY

To the GAUGE 'O' GUILD
. . . with gratitude

A scene on Ian Kings Grinling Junction layout .

MODEL
RAILWAYS
AND THEIR BUILDERS

BY
JACK RAY

TRANSPORT

Atlantic

PUBLISHERS

Introduction

SOME FOUR YEARS or so ago, I was fortunate in being able to persuade Jack Ray to let me have his first book 'A Lifetime with "O" Gauge' for publication and he was kind enough to ask me to write an introduction. I knew that the book would be well received and events have proved it, so it came as no surprise when he later told me that another idea had entered his ever-active mind and asked me whether I would be interested in looking at it and, if we went ahead, would I again write an introduction for him. Naturally I agreed and this new book is the result. What I had not expected was the sequence of events leading to the change of ownership of my old firm, but I am delighted that 'Atlantic' has gone into such good hands and that this latest offering from Jack is going ahead as first planned.

As before, this book breaks new ground and is an altogether more elaborate compilation than his previous title – but that is typical of the man himself; for he is no longer writing in a self-effacing manner about his own efforts. Instead, he has chosen to deploy his not inconsiderable literary skill to describe the efforts of other practitioners in the field. In consequence, he has given himself rather more latitude than when describing his own efforts and the benefit for us all is self-evident.

In these pages can be found fifty of the most influential railway modellers whom Jack has met over the years, along with their creative endeavours. Some of these folk are known to me personally; others I have, sadly, never encountered. But after reading Jack's account of their achievements I feel that I really do know all of them. It was simple in the case of those whom I had already met, for I recognised them instantly from Jack's description – which makes me absolutely certain that his account of the others whom I do not know is equally perceptive, accurate and affectionate.

In my introduction to his first book, I said ". . . Jack bears no sense of envy towards those whose skills exceed his own. But . . . his extraordinary capacity to 'turn an apposite phrase' and make his observations both readable and relevant, is just as important in the promotion of the hobby to a wider field as is any unique dexterity on the lathe or workbench."

If those remarks were valid in the context of Jack's own modelling, then they are even more applicable now he has chosen to describe the work of others; for this is an important book, make no mistake about that. How many of us have often wished that we knew more of the history of the well-known practitioners in our hobby than we do and looked in vain for a source of such information? Well, we need look no further – Jack has filled the gap and in doing so has made an immeasurably important contribution to the recorded history of our fascinating hobby. Unsurprisingly, the book reads like a good novel and on the final page one ends up wishing for much more – I can think of no finer recommendation.

David Jenkinson
Raskelf, North Yorkshire
April 1995

Published by Atlantic Transport Publishers
Trevithick House, West End, Penryn, Cornwall TR10 8HE

© Jack Ray, 1995

Unless otherwise credited, all photographs are by the author

ISBN: 0 906899 53 2

Layout and Design by Barry C. Lane, Sutton-in-Craven

Reproduction and printing by The Amadeus Press Ltd,
Huddersfield, West Yorkshire

British Cataloguing in Publication Data
A catalogue record for this book is available
from the British Library

CONTENTS

Preface

THE FAMILY of American tourists – father, mother, and two teenage children – sat at the next table in the large hotel restaurant, and even if their animated breakfast-time discussion had been conducted at normal conversational level it would have been clearly audible to the majority of other guests. Amused glances were cast at the family group as the now-familiar morning routine was followed, Mom armed with pencil and 'shopping list' of places to be visited, crossing off those already seen.

She hesitated.

"Hey, Elmer – have we done Stratford-on-Avon?"

The daughter chimed in eagerly. "Sure we have, Mom. You remember – that was the place where we went to that huge Macdonald's Eatery!"

The Immortal Bard having thus been cut down to size and disposed of, Mom cut another notch in her gun-butt by deleting Stratford from her list, while Pop added his confirmatory "Yeah – it was Toosday we went there. The carfee was terrible!"

Yet even as I smiled in amusement at this transatlantic obsession with being constantly on the move – seeing everything but seeing nothing – I felt some measure of empathy with them, for was I not doing something very similar as I roved the length and breadth of Britain, trying to cram into a brief thirty or forty minute audio-visual presentation the results of what was often a dedicated lifetime's work!

When I was approached by James Opie of the Railway Book Club, who asked me if I had ever considered putting into book form some of the riches I had gathered on these extensive travels, it helped me to crystalise an idea which had been mooted within the Gauge 'O' Guild for some time, with nothing actually being done about it. The problems were daunting, for although there were no purely legal problems (the copyright of any photograph being vested in the person who took it) there were considerations of courtesy and moral obligation to the Guild who had sponsored my journeys to a great extent. To my delight, the owners of the model railways I proposed to include all willingly gave their consent, and the Guild gave the project their blessing. Thus was my way made clear to start work.

My objectives were fairly clear in my mind – to present a cross-section of railway modellers, mainly in the field of Gauge 'O', but including other scales as well, with the emphasis on the people themselves rather than a technical treatise on how their railways were built, why they built them, and how they obtained the enjoyment and fulfilment they sought through this hobby. The last thing I wanted to do was to embark upon a qualitative comparison of the many and varied types of layout, for obviously standards of engineering and artistic excellence vary according to the skills, preferences, and amounts of time available to each modeller. Technical details of how these model railways were built are best left to textbooks and magazine articles. What always seems to be missing – except in obituaries – is a picture of the people themselves and what motivates them, for no two people approach the hobby from exactly the same angle. One man will spend a year or so building a superbly detailed and accurate model, with barely a thought about actually running it on a layout. Another concentrates on the fascinating science of signalling – the models themselves being of only secondary importance. Yet another will attempt to recreate in miniature some familiar scene of his younger days. There are scores of ways in which one may approach the hobby, every one of them equally valid, and to be measured only by the satisfaction they afford the owner.

My first apology – and explanation – must go to the many people who gave me full and willing permission to include their model railways, yet are not included in this book. The plain fact is that I am spoiled with riches – riches far beyond my capability to use. It all comes down to a question of balance, and the plethora of (for instance) LNER layouts of the 1930's, however fine they may be, would wreck that balance. So it is that a number of superb model railways have been omitted from these pages, and I would hasten to reassure the people who offered them that this is no reflection upon their merit; my gratitude for their cooperation is not one wit the less than for those whom I have included.

My grateful thanks go to my good friend, David Jenkinson who, as soon as I told him of James Opie's suggestion, agreed to publish the book. Health problems have since made it impossible for David to continue to run 'Atlantic', and although we regret this, it is equally true to say how pleased we all are that David's old friend, David Joy, has taken over the reins. He has enthusiastically continued where David Jenkinson left off, and what could have been a traumatic setback has proved to be an unusually smooth and amicable takeover.

My thanks also to the Gauge 'O' Guild in which and for which I have worked for the thirty-nine years of its existence, for without their goodwill and tangible support, very few of my photographic journeys would have been possible.

The 150-odd programmes I have made since 1980 have barely scratched the surface of this hobby, and these pages deal with only a small proportion of railway modellers I have visited. The hobby is about people – not things – and it is my hope that I have been able in some small way to bring some of these splendid people to you.

THE PIONEERS

John Hart

THE THING about John Hart's railway was that it worked. A fatuous comment, you may well think, for surely that is the purpose of a model railway – that it should function. Maybe, but there is all too often a yawning gap between purpose and achievement, and I have visited many a model railway which was in most respects superior to John's Midland & Southern Counties Joint Railway, but which was distinctly unreliable as to running. In order better to understand this extensive and complex model railway, running as it did through house and large garden, one has to look at the man behind it.

John Aubrey Hart, 1907-1979, son of a barrister, showed no inclination to follow his father's footsteps in Law, for his interests lay in the field of engineering. Upon leaving Tonbridge School he was articled to an engineering firm in Newbury, Berkshire, where he acquired a sound grounding in engineering. There followed a period when he served as a ship's engineer in the Merchant Navy, and a further spell when he worked for a firm of continental car manufacturers, all this taking place long before I knew him. Eventually, with the aid of a modest independent income bequeathed by his father, who died soon after the end of the 1939-45 war, he set up home with his one-time 'nanny', Miss Piper, who had come to the family as nursemaid when John was born. At the same time he started his own business as model-maker and repairer, using a spare bedroom in the house as his workshop. His mother seems to have been a somewhat vague figure who left the household while John was still an infant, and he had scarcely any recollection of her. His father, too – a successful barrister – would appear to have been so preoccupied by his profession that, apart from providing for his son's education and upbringing mainly, one imagines, at the hands of Miss Piper, a prep and then Public School, concerned himself little with his son.

In 1912, at the age of five, John was given a model of a L&SWR 0-4-4T engine, almost certainly the initial spur which drove him on to make model railways a hobby. That engine, still in its L&SWR livery, was still running on John's railway 67 years later when he died.

During the mid-1950s John formed a partnership with another model engineer, Rob Dettmar, the primary aim being to undertake model locomotive building and repairs, and to develop what John christened the RM motor. John very much admired the old Reid-Maxwell motor, but modified and considerably improved its design. Apart from the pole-pieces and magnets, the RM Motor was entirely hand-built in John's workshop, making production a slow and hopelessly uneconomic proposition, and building up a long waiting list for customers. Added to this, John would run a mile rather than pick up a pen, so he lost many potential customers, but his RM motors are still very much in use today and many owners regard them as the Rolls Royce of Gauge 'O' motors. Even the great Stanley Norris was so impressed by this motor that he commissioned John to replace all his own Rocket motors with the RM.

It was also during the 1950s that Rob Dettmar and John set up a public exhibition Gauge 'O' railway at Chessington Zoo in Surrey – the first such railway to use stud-contact electrical pickup. This venture soon foundered, for both Rob and John found that the revenue they obtained from the exhibition failed to recompense them for the lost income on their normal business.

Midland Railway 'flat-iron' 0-6-4T with tinplate clerestory carriages.

Meantime, John had built an extensive Gauge 'O' railway in his house and garden, using the 'outside-third' method of electrical pick-up. It was this railway which I described as a 'railway which worked', the reason being that not only was John's basic engineering thoroughly sound, but he operated a system of maintenance which meant that every locomotive and vehicle passed periodically through 'shops' and was fully tested. In this he was assisted by a growing band of youngsters who came to operate the Midland & Southern Counties Joint Railway. It is noteworthy that this railway ran a highly intensive timetable service several times each week throughout a period of some thirty years, and although attended by the usual minor faults which bedevil any model railway, was nevertheless basically sound and in full running order when he died.

In 1960 a further distraction threatened the continuance of the MSCJR when John joined the newly formed 'Bluebell Railway' in Sussex, becoming its principal driver. As with everything else he did, he threw himself heart and soul into this father of all restored railways, and on the days when he was on duty he would rise at 5am, motor-cycle – summer and winter – the 35 miles to Sheffield Park to take charge of his engine. His first charge was the little Wainwright 'P' class 0-6-0T, on which occasionally I would fire to him for a day, but when later the Bluebell took possession of the beautiful little Adams 'radial' 4-4-2T, John's name was painted up in the cab as the principal driver. John spent many hours on this engine, and quite a lot of ill-afforded money on bringing the engine up to the highest possible standards, travelling to Sheffield Park even in winter to work on his beloved Adams. The end came in the 1960 s when the autocratic general manager of the line (who was soon afterwards voted off the Board!) decreed that as there were more drivers waiting for work than there were engines for them to drive, the day must be shared. This meant that John would have to rise early, drive all that way to Sheffield Park, fire his engine and clean it, after which he would be allowed to take the first train of the day at 11am up to Horstead Keynes and back, and then hand the engine over to someone else who had never laid a hand on it in the way of maintenance, and who would drive it for the rest of the day. This intolerable situation caused John to part company with the Bluebell, and he returned to his first love – his Gauge 'O' model railway at his home in Surbiton.

During 1956 I had written an article in the Model Railway News, then under the aegis of J.N. Maskelyne, describing my own Crewchester Model Railway, and John had seen it. Realising that here was another man who was doing almost exactly the same as himself, that is, operating a Gauge 'O' garden railway with the help of a band of young lads, he wrote one of the only two letters I ever had from him in 25 years' friendship, asking if he may bring a band of his boys to Ipswich to visit Crewchester. Thus was formed a bond not only between the two clubs, but between John and myself, the effects of which were far reaching. Right up to the time of his death, the two clubs would exchange frequent visits, even though 90 miles separated us, and whenever I worked in Surrey or Kent, I would make John's house my base, staying there from Monday to Friday. His housekeeper, Miss Piper, died in 1961, leaving John to fend for himself, and as the house was entailed under his father's will, and would never be his absolute

property, John saw no reason to spend money on its upkeep, with the inevitable result that it began to fall to bits.

He never married, which was curious, for women found him attractive; indeed, he possessed more than his fair share of charm, and the mothers of the boys who spent much time in his house felt that their sons were safe in his hands, as indeed they were. He became a frequent weekend visitor to my own home where he was treated as one of the family, and his influence on Crewchester, both personally and practically, was immeasurable. For instance, he took most of my locomotives, one at a time, and fitted scale bogies in place of the crude pattern supplied by the makers — and did many other jobs to 'improve the breed'.

John would never say "You should do this — or that" — it was always a gentle "Have you tried so-and-so?" and invariably his suggested remedy solved the problem. If however the work was beyond the limited capabilities of the owner he would say "All right — leave it with me, I'll see what I can do." One would have to be patient, for time meant nothing to John, but in due course the engine would be handed back to its owner with "Try that. If it does not work, bring it back and we'll have another go." It always did work. Even today, Eddie Bye, whom I first met at John's house, and who learned his first engineering skills from John, tells me that he finds himself working on a job, is tempted to cut a corner or skimp some part, and there is the vision of John sitting at his shoulder, like the Cheshire cat in Alice, his moustache revolving slowly and a frown on his brow, and causing Eddie to say "Drat you, John!" and start the job again, doing it as John would have done it.

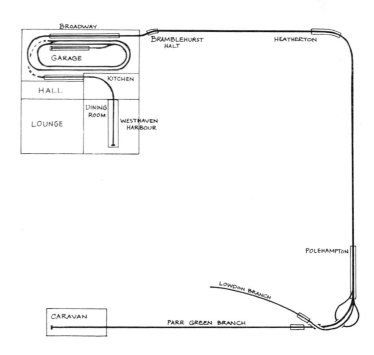

The Midland & Southern Counties Joint Railway.

John built two 'West Country' underframes, one electric and one clockwork for Derek Lucas who built the bodies for the locomotives.

He always described himself as 'an engineering hack', which was selling himself short, for he was far more than that, and there must be many modellers who owe John a debt of gratitude for the help he gave them. Although not perhaps aspiring to the superlative standards of his friend, Bernard Miller, or Stanley Beeson, John's work was always the very best he could do – which was very good indeed.

As with any complex character, John had almost contradictory facets to his personality, and there were clear traces of the 'Upstairs-Downstairs' way of life from his youth, with a touch of arrogance strangely at odds with his warm and generous nature, this trait often manifesting itself in his dealings with tradesmen. He found it hard to adapt himself to the post-war egalitarian society where Jack is (allegedly) as good as his master.

I would like to end with two anecdotes in which John was concerned. One day Eddie Bye brought him a problem engine which, despite all his efforts, he just could not run successfully. John took the engine from Eddie, adjusted his magnifying spectacles, and thoroughly inspected every part of it. He attached two leads and ran the motor for a few seconds, and then sat back again, thoughtfully regarding the loco for some slow-moving minutes. One just did not interrupt such seances – one just waited quietly. After a long pause, John reached down to a tool rack

beside his bench, extracted a small hammer, placed it carefully on part of the chassis, and then suddenly gave it a sharp tap.

"There, Eddie" he said "Try that."

The engine has been trouble-free from then to this day!

The other story concerns an engine which I bought from John Hart, quite unknown to Eddie Bye. Some twenty years later Eddie offered to take that engine home with him to do some work on it, and having done so, phoned me one evening.

"That Drummond Castle – has it ever been through John Hart's hands?"

"Why do you ask?"

"I don't really know – but as I worked on that engine I thought I felt John's workmanship all over it – it seems to carry his trademark everywhere."

Many a man – far more illustrious than John – has lived and died, bequeathing less to posterity.

THE PIONEERS

Norman Eagles

I N 1951, WHEN the name Crewchester was first coined, Norman Eagles' Sherwood Section of the L.M.S. had been established thirty years, and it was to last a further thirty before the last train ran into Nottingham Castle station. It is almost impossible for me to write purely objectively of Norman, for although we met but seldom in the years 1951 to 1981, we shared a common addiction to clockwork propulsion. Norman was by common consent recognised as the uncrowned king of clockwork.

Although Norman and I shared this preference for spring-drive (the posh name for clockwork), there were great differences in our respective railways, for at a time when I was running Hornby and Bassett Lowke locomotives, Norman was using scratch-built models of a very high standard indeed. He had around him a band of devoted operators who met regularly to run an extremely taxing timetable which demanded considerable skill, experience, and sheer mental concentration. Among these was Ken Brennan whose railway is featured elsewhere in this book.

The aspect of the Sherwood lines which impressed me most, I think, was the way Norman and his merry men had overcome one of the principal bugbears of clockwork – the problem of introducing a clockwork mechanism into small engines, especially low-boilered types. One member of the Sherwood team had perfected a method of so modifying the mechanism by relocating the driving axles as to lower the height of the spring which protruded from the top of the mainframes and thus demanded a high boiler-line. The result was a collection of engines ranging from big Pacifics down to small tanks, a very rare sight on a spring-driven system. One engine in particular caught my eye – a beautifully detailed Kirtley 'curly-frame' 0-6-0 with a wealth of detail.

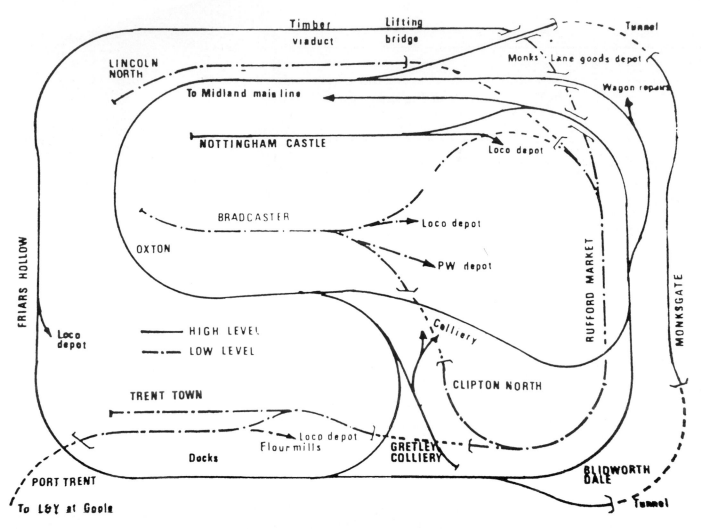

Timber viaduct
Lifting bridge
Tunnel
LINCOLN NORTH
Monks Lane goods depot
To Midland main line
Wagon repairs
NOTTINGHAM CASTLE
Loco depot
BRADCASTER
Loco depot
OXTON
PW depot
FRIARS HOLLOW
RUFFORD MARKET
MONKSGATE
Loco depot
HIGH LEVEL
LOW LEVEL
Colliery
CLIPTON NORTH
TRENT TOWN
Loco depot
Flour mills
Docks
GRETLEY COLLIERY
BLIDWORTH DALE
PORT TRENT
Tunnel
To L&Y at Goole

Comparatively few people were able to view this famous line for the simple reason that there was barely sufficient room for the operators – let alone visitors. I did not ever visit the railway in its earlier home in Pinner, and even when it was moved to its new large purpose-built 'shed' in his large garden there was still little room for spectators. So complex was the time-table that even when we made the Guild programme it was impossible to move any of the trains or stock to pose for photographs, for that would throw the whole system into chaos for the next running session. These sessions – once weekly affairs – had, by the time I went there, changed to monthly events. The sheer burden of mainten-ance of such a system was proving almost too much for Norman's ad-vanced years, but the railway was still in full running order. Even so, I was able to photograph the entire railway as it would appear at 5am – before the first trains of the day started moving.

I suppose one of the most frequently heard critical comments in the heyday of Norman Eagles' railway was concerning the track, and I have to admit to joining this criticism. "Why" people often asked "does Norman never use ballast on his track?" Having been laid long before the advent of so-called fine-scale, the track was proprietary (steel) bullhead, supported by chairs on timber sleepers at about 2in intervals. It was laid with great care and accuracy, but when juxtaposed to the delicate detail of the station buildings it reminded one of a crude pen-and-ink sketch laid on a Constable landscape. During the early years of our acquaintance I had avoided asking the question for fear of giving offence, but when in 1982 I went to Norman's home to make the Guild programme I felt I knew him well enough to broach the subject. His answer was given in his characteristic, forthright manner.

"It is a subject which has often been mooted" he told me "but there are two very practical reasons why ballast has never been introduced on this railway. Firstly, the sheer weight of ballast on this vast area of baseboard would threaten it with collapse, and secondly, all the signals are operated from the frames by means of threads running through eyelets screwed into the baseboard. The job of raising these on battens, even if it were practicable, is well beyond me at my time of life." With that I had to be content, and indeed accepted his explanation completely.

I have remarked elsewhere in this book how often I find these model railwaays are in some way interlinked, sometimes apparently quite incongruously. For instance – with the very greatest respect for Norman's railway – it seemed remarkable that Norman had acquired several items of scenery from the late W.S. Norris layout – a railway which in its time was the very epitome of 7mm fine-scale modelling. The Red Lion Inn at Oxton on the

Sherwood line came from the Norris railway, as did some cattle-docks. Norman was also a great friend of Geoff. Bigmore (of Bigston fame). Ken Brennan, who has already been mentioned in this chapter, did the original drawings for both the Sherwood layouts. Ken's own building of the maltings later became incorporated in the Sherwood backdrop, and after Norman's death, reverted to Ken once again.

Memories are notoriously short, and already, less than a decade since Norman died, a generation has grown up who have never even heard the name of Norman Eagles, yet for over sixty years Sherwood graced the pages of model railway journals, written in the fluent way Norman had, and with many pictures. Sherwood is a major part of model railway history, and must have influenced countless aspiring modellers – including myself for one.

I have mentioned that many of the locomotives on the Sherwood line were far smaller than one would normally expect to find on a clockwork system, and that the mechanisms had been 'doctored' so as to fit into the low-boilered types. I am indebted once again to Ken Brennan for supplying me with the name of that ingenious man – it was Leslie Forrest – alias WINDSOR MODELS.

It is said that a man may be known by the company he keeps, and Norman certainly surrounded himself with a company of very talented men until well beyond the time when clockwork was the most popular propulsion for model trains, all of them prepared to exercise their several skills to the furtherance of this huge railway system. But every army depends for its success on the General who holds it together by his own intiative, drive, and even leadership. Such a man was Norman Eagles. With his passing one of the giants of Gauge 'O' fell, and is missed.

Harold Bower

THE STORY of the Gauge 'O' Guild's genesis has been related in some detail in my book "A LIFETIME WITH 'O' GAUGE" and while it is not my intention to repeat the circumstances which led to the formation of the Guild here, nevertheless Harold Bower's part was so vitally important that it would be unthinkable to omit reference to it in any book about the Guild. Suffice it to say that in 1956, at a time when Gauge 'O' seemed to be heading for oblivion, it was Harold who convened that first meeting which led to the formation of the now thriving organisation we see today.

But this book is not concerned with the history of the Guild; rather is it an account of railway modellers of all kinds, and their activities. Harold Bower is one of those people who seem destined to lead, and it was fortuitous for those of us who clung desperately to our chosen gauge that the hour produced the man. Whatever part the rest of us played in our several roles, it was Harold who, as it were, turned the first sod – and to continue the metaphor, tended the garden during its first seven or eight formative years. As the Guild's first chairman I naturally met Harold for those first few tentative committee meetings, held usually in Harold's home. At that time he had a garden railway in 'O' Gauge, and my clearest recollection of those days in 1956/57 is of finding in a junk shop in Chelmsford a Hornby No. 2 special 4-4-0 in Southern livery, of the L1 class. I paid all of £2 for this, but as my own railway was predominantly LNER/LMS the Southern Railway loco was out of place, I passed it on to Harold for the same princely sum. (Today, that same engine would carry a price tag with at least two 0's added to it!).

Being a man who refused to be confined by restrictive boundaries, Harold experimented with other gauges – notably 00, and even today he has in his house a very ambitious 00 railway, in addition to the large and complex 7mm system, but his main allegiance remains wtih 'O' gauge. Once the Guild had found its feet, Harold handed over the reins to others and for many years he remained somewhat in the background of events. His extensive travels in Europe took him frequently to the Austro-German border country and the Karwendel mountains where he formed not only great affection for the railways there but became very knowledgable about them. Upon moving to a large house with extensive cellars he perceived the opportunity to create a system based on the railways he had come to know so well, and his ingenious mind devised a complex system embracing railway links between such places as Innsbruck, Hoch Zirl, Seffeld, Mitten-wald, Garmisch, Arlberg and Murnau, with the branch to Oberammergau.

The locale of this model railway was unusual to say the least and anyone taller than a Hobbit would be well-advised to wear a steel helmet, for the roof was often less than 5ft from the earthen floor. The line did in fact pass out briefly into the garden, but the greater part of it was in a series of Troglodite rooms in the cellars. Scenery was skilfully placed behind the railway wherever possible, and although I have never been to these places myself, I was well able to appreciate what they were like. The control system was ingenious, making it possible for one man to run the entire system. Taking the photographs proved far less difficult than I had imagined at first, although some contortions were necessary at times.

In making the programme, Harold was able to provide some really fine colour pictures of the prototype, from which I made slides to be included in the presentation.

The original programme was made in 1985, but, following extensive modifications and improvements, Harold invited me to go there again in 1992 to make an entirely new programme, although the original has been retained in the Collection for the sake of comparison. Altogether, a most refreshing change from the usual British layouts, and a most entertaining programme.

Bound up in the history of evolution of this hobby are a few outstanding key-figures – men of vision and initiative who took action which in greater or less degree affected the whole course of the hobby. Certainly, the apparently dying embers of Gauge 'O' were stirred into a blaze by the efforts of Harold Bower, and the ensuing conflagration has surprised even the most optimistic members who supported Harold in those early days.

Rex Stedman

DAVID PEACOCK

Stedman Trust

A SMALL CHILD had just learned that Father Christmas was a myth, and in an agony of disillusionment he wept, crying bitterly "There's no Santa Claus – there's no God – there's no Devil – it's all DADDY!"

In our younger days there seemed to be certain things which were immutable and eternal, such as summer and winter, day and night, school, and rice pudding. To these, every boy of my generation would add Hornby, Bassett-Lowke, and Leeds Model Co. When, in later years I watched the demise, one by one, of these pillars of permanence, I felt great sympathy for that young lad who had lost his innocent belief in Santa Claus. The trouble is that these giants who bestrode the world of model railways in its early evolution are apt to be quickly forgotten once their generation has passed away, and were it not for a handful of dedicated chroniclers who write books, reprint old catalogues, and in other ways try to present things as they were, the facts would become blurred, distorted, or even lost completely.

David Peacock has taken a very unusual course of action in establishing a Trust (of which he is now sole proprietor) of the products of the Leeds Model Company, who from 1912 to well after the Second World War were a mainstay of the world of model railways, specially in that of Gauge 'O'. But, instead of merely writing articles on the history of this company and the remarkable man who founded it, Rex Stedman, David has ranged the whole realm of model railways, acquiring examples of L.M.C. products, and it would be fair to say that there is probably no-one today who is a greater authority on this subject than he, when one considers the vast range of LMC products (there were nearly 90 goods wagons!) and realises that David has examples of almost every one, beside the locomotives and coaches produced by LMC.

David Peacock tells the story of Rex Stedman and the Leeds Model Company in the Gauge 'O' Guild programme, and it is not the purpose of this brief chapter to reproduce the fascinating tale here, but I can offer a summary of the firm which has not only played such a vital part in the evolution of the hobby of model railways, but has preoccupied David Peacock for many years. Although the Trust is a thoroughly well organised project, it is not primarily a profit-making concern; David is a professional metallurgist, and this Trust is very much a hobby. There must be many people of my generation – and possibly latter-day collectors – who have turned to David for items or parts from the one-time Leeds catalogue, and found what they sought. For instance, I have a very ancient Leeds Sentinel rail-car named NETTLE, the exterior being in litho-printed paper. My own Sentinel became very badly scarred, with parts of the litho missing, and David was able to furnish me with a fresh set.

Rex Stedman started up in business as a model railway manufacturer in 1912, the Company actually being started by G.P. Keen, who was its Chairman, after which (much later) Rex himself took over. After the Second World War ownership passed yet again into various hands, until the Company was finally wound up. Rex Stedman's son, Adrian, who was tragically killed in a car accident, was himself very much concerned with his father's firm, and it was friendship with David Peacock which led ultimately to David's "Leeds Stedman Trust."

So what exactly is the purpose and function of the Trust? I suppose that primarily it is like any other hobby involving the seeking out and collecting of some specific product, be it postage stamps, match-boxes, or beer-mats – the joy is in the chase, the discovery of a genuine Leeds Model Co. product, and then acquiring ownership of it. Because LMC products were all of good quality, many examples survive and are still in regular use by owners of model railways. Travelling round the country, photographing layouts I am constantly coming across examples of two Leeds locomotives – the little Lancashire & Yorkshire 2-4-2T and the equally ubiquitous Robinson 4-4-0 'Director' – still very much in running order, and cherished by their owners. Many such examples are lost after the death of their owners when executors of Wills, ignorant of their value, dispose of them to junk dealers just to clear the house, and I have known cases where a collection was – on the advice of the solicitors – consigned to the local rubbish tip.

One of David's principal delights in operating this Trust, is to come across an item of LMC such as, for instance, a model of BUTLER HENDERSON, one of the Directors produced by that firm, which has become damaged and the paintwork all but destroyed, and lovingly restored it to its original condition. In doing this he encounters some of the collector-purists who hold up their hands in horror, telling him what he is doing is almost vandalism! But what these people completely fail to appreciate is that this is exactly how those models were treated by the manufacturer; they were hand-painted individually and hand-lined. The cost of such labour, even in those far-off days, meant that Rex Stedman had to sail very close to the wind financially, and it was not at all uncommon for a model locomotive to go out on sale, un-numbered, simply to save the cost of transfers! So David is doing exactly what Stedman did when the models were first built.

We have come to regard the use of plastics in the manufacture of models as very much a feature of post 39-45 war years, but Stedman was using an early form of plastic, called Bakelite, as far back as 1925 to build his coaches.

It seems to me that his Leeds Stedman Trust is a most fitting companion to similar organisations such as The Hornby Collectors' Association, the Bassett Lowke Society, et al, for there is no doubt that the Leeds Model Company was a vitally important part of the evolution of this hobby of model railways, Rex Stedman taking his place alongside W.J. Bassett-Lowke, Geoffrey Keen, and Frank Hornby.

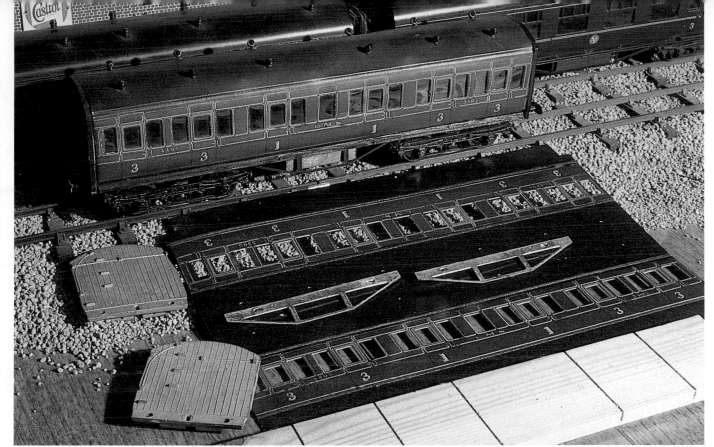

Some of the earliest kits were these LMS parts which made very attractive models.

Private owner wagons included many popular and colourful liveries in addition to this own prototype example.

The LNER teak coaches are very rare and now most collectable. The bodies were Bakelite and not as heavy as the normal wooden coaches of the period.

John Anning

GOG Slide collection No. 70

TODAY, with the hobby of model railways thriving, and almost every town and city in Britain boasting at least one model railway club, group, or association, I sometimes wonder what the younger generation would make of a statement such as "John Anning was for many years Chairman – and later President – of The Model Railway Club."

"Oh yes?" they reply, "– which model railway club?"

This, to my generation, is rather like a soldier saying that his Regiment was The Blues, and then being asked, "Oh yes? Which blues?" Going back some sixty years when Geoffrey Keen was so active in helping the early days of The Model Railway Club (note the upper case initials!) there would be no confusion over the name, for, with one or two notable exceptions, such organisations just did not exist, so the title required no amplification. And so it has remained until today, its unadorned title standing like the brass plate discreetly displayed outside an exclusive hatter in St. James, "LOCK'S OF ST. JAMES."

A succession of distinguished names have filled high office in this club, with G.P. Keen occupying the Chair for some thirty years (after which he became President), followed later by John Anning who held both these coveted appointments. In fact, it was during John's 16 years' tenure of the Chair that the plans were laid leading to the building of the London Headquarters of the Model Railway Club, John himself supervising the entire process. This building was understandably named Keen House, and it was here that for some eight or nine years of its early life the Gauge 'O' Guild (which is affiliated to the MRC) held its meetings until it was forced to seek larger premises. It was at one of those early meetings at Keen House that I remember someone pointing out John Anning to me, explaining that he was the Club's Chairman, but it was not until some thirty years later that I met John personally at Geoffrey Keen's house. It was on that occasion that we made arrangements for me to visit John's own layout so that I may add this to the rapidly developing Guild collection of audio-visual programmes.

Naturally, I was intrigued to discover what sort of railway such a distinguished man had built, and I was not to be disappointed. It was in fact the next programme I made after visiting G.P. Keen's railway, where the photographic results were somewhat disappointing. I may mention in parenthesis that the problems had not entirely disappeared when I photographed John's railway, and this led me to take the camera in for examination by an expert, where it was discovered that the shutter was working at least one stop faster than it should. Such are the perils lurking in the path of the amateur!

However, there were no excuses of poor lighting on John's railway, for much of it lay in the open, the total run extending 110 feet, starting in the garage (where else!) and running to the bottom of the garden. The line, built at table top height for most of its length, represented a fictional extension of the Southern Railway, and passed through one main intermediate station, housed in a large shed, before continuing to a final shed at the bottom of the garden. Owing to a slight rise in the ground, that far shed contained a terminus which was nearer to the ground than at the garage end. There also was the small terminus of a branch line, worked on that day by a delightful push-pull train.

The stations and their environs left one in no doubt about their source of inspiration, for they were clearly of Southern architecture, and beautifully detailed, and this was specially true of the intermediate station. All bore names suggesting the locality where John lived, which is very much Southern territory, and indeed John grew up in Dover to be precise, where as a boy he saw many types of Southern train in the three stations there – Priory, Marine, and Harbour.

Whilst it is not the purpose of these pages to embark upon a detailed description of that railway, certain features stand out in my memory. For instance, a very fine model of a Schools class 4-4-0 had been presented to John by the grateful Model Railway Club in recognition of his considerable efforts in supervising the planning and construction of Keen House during his Chairmanship of the Club. His sixteen years in that office had inevitably resulted in him having little time to continue his own model building, and by way of partial compensation, the Club had presented him with a fine set of Maunsell coaches.

One of the eternal problems of the outdoor modeller is the weather, and John had provided a series of shelters made from perspex which could be installed in showery conditions, and removed when not needed. These gave a great measure of protection to the trains along that outdoor section, thereby permitting operation in poor weather.

Being keenly interested in signals, especially semaphores, I was struck by the fine examples of such items on John's railway, and he told me that some of these had been built by his son-in-law. (I remember commenting to John at the time that he must have brought his daughter up very well.) Her husband, Barry Harper, had built two superb gantries, one of which stood outside in the garden, plus a very striking sky-arm co-acting signal at the approaches to the intermediate station.

The railway was operated principally on the stud-contact system of current collection, but, being Southern, it was not surprising to see an outside third juice rail, and John told me that four of his trains took their power from this. In addition to the steam-outline locomotives, there were several emu's with their curious mnemonic initials.

With such a distinguished track-record, John can hardly be accused of a frivolous approach to the hobby, but, behind the dedicated attitude lies a man of considerable, somewhat dry humour, which I find enormously refreshing in a hobby where so many people tend to be suspicious of anything less than reverence. Brief glimpses of this humour had been revealed to me when we were working together on Geoffrey Keen's railway, and in which I perceived something of a kindred spirit.

So it was that I was not altogether surprised when, upon asking John for something unusual with which to finish the programme, he brought out four tank-wagons, each of which was very professionally painted by one of his group, and bore the name of its company on one side, while the opposite side of the tanks displayed some VERY curious legends! Just as I brought the Guild programme to a close with pictures of these, so I end this chapter with the following:
LIQUID FUDGE
REDLAND ROOF SOLVENT (The imagination boggles at the use of this!)
GLACIER FLUID
RUNNIE MEAD   ALES AND STOUT.

THE PIONEERS
Geoffrey Keen

ONE DAY in 1986 I had a telephone call from Derek Lucas.
"Had you heard" he asked me "that Mrs. Keen is having to dispose of their model railway? She is now into her nineties and is having problems with her sight, as a result of which she finds it impossible to keep the railway going. I wondered if this might be of interest to you?"

Derek must have caught me on a bad day, for there were one or two words in his enquiry which puzzled me. He had referred to this railway as 'their' railway, suggesting joint ownership. A club? A family? Then again, the name 'Mrs. Keen' did not ring any immediate bell in my mind, and anyway, did Derek imagine I was in a financial position to purchase unwanted model railways?

Further conversation with Derek nudged my somewhat sluggish memory, and eventually the penny dropped. There was in the Gauge 'O' Guild a Life Honorary member named Mrs. Keen, and such privileges are not lightly bestowed by the Guild, but I had never met Mrs. Keen, nor her illustrious husband, Geoffrey Keen who died in 1973, and after whom the London Headquarters of the Model Railway Club had been named. I knew that Geoffrey Keen had been an influential figure in the world of model railways, but, to my shame, I did not know that Mrs. Keen herself was actively involved in the hobby, having her own Gauge

'O' model railway called The Pantry Dockyard Railway. Keen's own railway was known as The K Lines, and since his death the entire collection had been maintained by Mrs. Keen. It was this that she was having to dispose of, and the reason for Derek's phone call was not to suggest that I might be interested in buying all or part of it (that was to be handled by Christie's) but that I might feel like making some record of the railway before it was too late.

I assured Derek that I most certainly was, and that if he could give me Mrs. Keen's address, I would contact her with a view to making a Guild audio/visual programme. I received an immediate response to my letter, suggesting one or two suitable dates, and we agreed a day in February 1986. I was invited to spend the day there, and as she was not enjoying the best of eyesight, she felt it might be beyond her to act as my guide for such an ambitious project, so she had invited John Anning to be present. This was indeed a bonus, for although I knew of John, so far as I could remember we had never met, even though we must have both been present at meetings at Keen House.

BENE STALK was a freelance design 0-4-0 tank based on several prototypes and thus rather familiar in appearance. The name was Keen's joke with his wife.

I had been given an address in Hythe, Kent, a town I knew well, so the route there was a familiar one. The journey was, to put it mildly, memorable, for during the past week heavy snow had fallen, causing many minor roads to become impassable, and even the trunk routes were hazardous in places, especially over the Downs. Further snow was forecast. Periods of blue sky and brilliant winter sunshine alternated with low, black clouds racing in from the east, bringing with them blinding blizzards which reduced visibility almost to nil and bringing my progress down to a crawl, after which the sun would appear again, bathing the countryside and its freshly fallen coating of snow in dazzling light.

The approach to the house was up a steep hill which fortunately had been gritted, and which took me up to a road running high above the cliffs between Hythe and Folkestone, overlooking the Channel, although with the the threat of another heavy squall looming over the sea, I did not linger to view the magnificent seascape. The house was itself stood on this lofty eminence, the door being opened to me by Mrs. Keen herself, and any picture I may have formed in my mind of a frail, bent, little old lady was quickly dispelled, for she was anything but that. The years had dealt kindly with Geoffrey Keen's widow, for she was erect, alert, and in full command not only of herself, but of the situation. A welcoming greeting was followed by a quick appraisal of the gathering blizzard, whereupon she suggested that I may like to get my gear inside the front door before the weather made it impossible, and this I did.

Once inside, I was introduced properly to John Anning, who had wasted no time on small-talk, but helped me with the equipment before we rejoined Mrs. Keen in the beautiful lounge where we had a welcome cup of coffee. At the far end of this room was a large picture window which gave on to the sea, and, Mrs. Keen told me, in good visibility one looked straight into Boulogne harbour. At the moment, however, thick snow obscured everything. After telling us that lunch would be ready at about 1 p.m. our hostess came with us to the railway room, explaining that John would be far better able to answer any questions I might want to ask as he had for many years been closely associated with her husband, both on the K Lines and in the Model Railway Club.

We were then left to our own devices, and very quickly I found that John was an ideal companion for this venture, so much so that I had the feeling we had known each other for quite a while instead of this being our first meeting. From John – and later, Don Boreham, I was able to glean much information about the man who had built this railway, Geoffrey P. Keen, 1889-1973. He was a wealthy businessman with considerable interests on the continent; he spoke French fluently, and the continental influence was clearly reflected in his models. Although a man blessed with great organisational gifts, he was of a retiring nature, shunning the limelight, and preferring to do much good by stealth. He was Chairman of Bassett Lowke's, and financed Rex Stedman in the formation of The Leeds Model Company, of which he was a Director. Under his influence and support, the Model Railway Club grew and flourished, Keen being its Chairman for thirty years, and later, President. It was little wonder therefore that the new Headquarters in London was named Keen House!

The railway room itself contained table-top baseboard running along both sides and across the far end, the entire area covered by a mass of trackwork, much of which was occupied by a bewildering array of locomotives, coaches, and wagons. I have to admit that for a very amateur photographer, with limited equipment and even more limited expertise, the room presented formidable problems, for it was lit by normal house lighting, but this was constantly changing with the light which came from the window – one moment throwing great shafts of low sunlight across the room, and the next moment blotted out by yet another squall. Flood-lamps did little to help, for my light-meters developed a sort of St Vitus dance as they tried vainly to discover a stable light value.   A poor workman always blames his tools. I wish now that it were possible to return, armed with greater experience and improved equipment, but at the time I was up against the imminent dispersal of the railway.

John Anning worked tirelessly helping me by posing various items where I could reach them with my camera, and making notes for the commentary we would record later. It has to be borne in mind that these recorded commentaries have to be made when the pictures are still in the camera, so meticulous notes of the content of each shot have to be made. Several things on that railway stand out vividly in my memory.

Firstly there was the magnificent LNER 2-8-0 + 0-8-2 Beyer-Garratt built for Keen by Rex Stedman, and which is now in the National Railway Museum. Then my eye was taken by a big Belgian Pacific locomotive with outside cylinders and valve-gear, the curious feature of which was that each side of that engine had a different form of valve-gear! (Shades of Webb!).

One little 0-4-0T shunter bore the name BENE STALK (sic), the reason being that in their younger days, Keen's pet-name for his wife had been 'Bean-stalk'. The extensive collection of freight vehicles reminded me slightly of Dr. Scott's N.E. layout in its astonishing variety. A series of flat wagons carried the vast barrel of a naval gun, just as Bob Scott's line had. Scattered all over this collection of railway locomotives and rolling stock were many painted in the distinctive livery and lettering of The Pantry Dockyard Railway, Mrs. Keen's own domain. No railway-widow

was this remarkable lady; her railway alone would be the envy of any enthusiast.

And here I would stress that in the days when this model railway was planned and built, fine-scale was virtually unheard of, yet such was the standard of engineering on all the models that they would stand up to close comparative study alongside today's best. Keen himself was an accomplished engineer, and indeed was very much connected with Winteringham's, the engineering side of Bassett Lowke, of which firm he was Chairman.

Another feature stands out in my memory – a signal lever frame of some 80 levers, the remarkable part of it being the fully-inter-locking mechanical frame of tappet bars which lay below and behind the levers themselves. It was a little miracle of miniature engineering, and I could well have spent an hour or more learning the intricacies of that interlocking frame.

It would be impossible to attempt even this brief summary of that remarkable railway without reference to the wagon-lits, for they carried an amusing story. Keen had commissioned a set of wagons-lit from a noted French model-maker, Paschal Rossy, a man not exactly famous for the speed of his work, so the coaches were delivered one at a time as they became ready. They were superb examples of the model-maker's craft, beautifully finished

both as to exterior and interior, and indeed, the interior tended to distract attention from the exterior! Every sleeping compartment was fully detailed with luxurious decor, beds, washbasins, etc., but M. Rossy had added (unbidden by Keen) further embellishments in the form of extremely curvaceous young ladies in various stages of their toilettes. It has to be remembered that this was long before OMEN FIGURES started to issue their range of girlies – and even before the so-called 'permissive age' had broken! Keen – being no prude (nor indeed was his wife) – accepted the vehicle, not without amusement, but instructed M. Rossy that further coaches need not include such exotic (and erotic) detail. Paschal Rossy, however, had different ideas, and obviously, for him, a wagon-lit was not a wagon-lit until it contained these refugees from the Folies Bergeres. The remainder of the contract was duly fulfilled, complete with its complement of nubile wenches, all of which were accepted with philosophical fortitude by Mr. and Mrs. Keen. It was noticeable that when I visited the railway the train had been marshalled with the windows of the sleeping compartments facing outwards from that horseshoe layout, doubtless in case the nearby Archbishop of Canterbury might look in unexpectedly. In order to see this other side of the train it was necessary to drop onto one's hands and knees and make a

back-breaking trip to reach the far side. (My own back recovered in less than a week).

During lunch, which was taken in that lounge, and from which now a magnificent view of the Channel was possible, Mrs. Keen told me ruefully "My husband did comment that he seemed to be involved in super-detail models in more ways than one!"

That phone call from Derek Lucas had quite a remarkable chain-reaction, for not only did it lead to my meeting a most remarkable lady, but also to get to know John Anning; indeed, it was on that occasion that John and I made arrangements for me to visit his own model railway in order to make a Guild programme on that.

I have to admit that the photographic results of that one visit to the 'K Lines' were disappointing (for which I alone am to blame) but at least they were better than nothing. Geoffrey Keen was not one to seek publicity, and the records of his railway and indeed of his whole vital involvement in the early pioneering days of the hobby are somewhat sparse. Memories are notoriously short, and unless facts are recorded before they become obscured by time, they are soon lost. At least I was able to see much of what this venturesome man had accomplished, but I do wish I had been able to meet him.

Stanley Norris & Bernard Miller

I T IS DOUBTFUL if any one event in the history of Gauge 'O' railway modelling has had such a profound and lasting influence on the hobby as did the coming together of Bernard Miller and Stanley Norris. So inextricably interwoven are the stories of these two men that I am placing them together in this one section of my book. Although their personal backgrounds differed widely, Stanley Norris being a very wealthy man and Bernard Miller a practising model-maker, the catalyst of Gauge 'O' models fused them into an almost indivisible entity. It was my great good fortune to come to know both these remarkable men as friends.

Often heard within the hobby of model railways is the term 'Cheque-book modellers', usually employed in a somewhat disparaging manner, suggesting an idle dilettante who merely dabbles in the hobby, paying others to build his railway and then enjoy just the running of the trains. It is all too easy for those of us who are dedicated to the hobby to an almost obsessional degree to denigrate such people, but I would be inclined to argue their case, for they have just as valid a reason for their models as any other – the only yardstick being the enjoyment they derive from them. However, in Stanley Norris – wealthy though he undoubtedly was – there was no trace of the 'idle dilettante'. At the age of twelve he was already building model locomotives which would be the envy of many a man twice that age. The ultimate vast empire of Gauge 'O' railway which he owned was as much the result of his own craftsmanship and vision, as of anyone else involved.

Back in the nineteen-twenties, Norris – dissatisfied with the crude track parts supplied by the trade – had his own rail-section specially drawn for him, together with similarly scaled chairs, and this was long before the term 'fine-scale' had been coined. In his West Byfleet home he built a model railway which would bear comparison with many of today's finest Gauge 'O' railways, and which used the outside-third rail for current collection. Two-rail power supply had yet to be made commercially viable.

At about the time when Norris was building this amazing model railway of his, Bernard Miller was setting himself up in Wimbledon as a model engineer, and he too felt strongly that much could be done to improve standards, with closer-to-scale wheels and track. His pioneering efforts were far from universally welcomed, perhaps understandably so, for to someone with an extensive model railway, wholesale rebuilding of both stock and track would be necessary before he could embrace these new, finer, standards. Even when he went into partnership with Captain Swan, a motor-engineer who was specially interested in the electrical side of the trade, his partner was far from enthusiastic about Miller's intense desire to work to finer standards, and in fact did his best to persuade him to adopt the status quo. But Miller persisted, and had already built what was almost certainly the first-ever 'fine-scale' model locomotive, an LNWR 2-4-0 tender engine which, incidentally, is still running today.

During the 1930 s the firm of Miller Swan gained recognition among the more discerning modellers, and long before the 1939 war their catalogue offered all wheels in two standards – 28mm b-b or 29mm b-b, although even then the term 'fine-scale' had not been coined. As has been pointed out elsewhere, the words 'fine-scale' are a misnomer for it is nothing to do with scale. However, the name has become accepted and most people know what it implies.

It seemed almost inevitable that two such ardent advocates of these improved standards should meet, and shortly before the 1939 war that is exactly what happened. Norris heard of what Miller was doing and lost no time in contacting him, with the result that each immediately recognised in the other a kindred spirit. Thus was born an immortal association of minds and skills which has had such a tremendous effect on the development of Gauge 'O'. There was more to this than merely improved standards, for Miller was convinced that the 2-rail method of current collection was feasible, and was determined to pursue it, realising that if it could be made to work, the unsightly third rail could be eliminated and track consequently made to appear more like its prototype.

Unfortunately, the 1939 war intervened in the development of many hobbies, including model railways, and Miller's partner went off to rejoin the Army with the rank of Lt. Colonel, while Miller became heavily engaged in national defence work. He wound the firm up and in fact, so far as I know, the two men never met again.

With the cessation of hostilities, Bernard Miller quickly renewed his contact with Norris, who was, among many other things, a Director of Rocket Precision, a firm producing their own electric motors which Norris used for his own locomotives. For a while, Bernard Miller worked for Rocket Precision, until the time when Norris moved to a new estate in Surrey where he planned to build a quite fantastic Gauge 'O' model railway, housed in a large purpose-designed building some 72ft by 25ft, air-conditioned and heated. On this estate was a bungalow which he offered to Bernard, together with an honorarium which would not only enable him to pursue his modelling activities, but which gave Norris first call upon his services. The actual arrangement, I believe, was a minimum of two days per week, but this was flexible, neither party observing the agreement too rigidly. For instance, when visitors were due, Bernard was expected to be on hand to help operate the vast system.

The LB&SCR featured prominently. This station was named Stroudley.

N. Corner collection

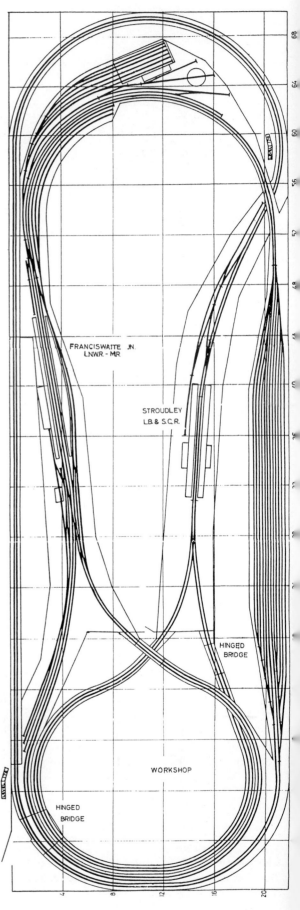

The LNWR side of the layout shared a section with the Midland and the name was derived from the christian names of two of those railway's CMEs.
N. Corner collection

The models themselves were of the highest standard but it was the fine scale trackwork that created the greatest impression when photographs of the layout first appeared in the 1950s. These views and the one overleaf emphasise the benefits of large radius curves and correct ballasting.

It was during the development of this huge model railway that I first came on to the scene, via the good offices of John Hart, whose RM motor had attracted Norris enormously. In fact, so impressed was Norris with the RM motor that he commissioned John to go through his entire stud of locomotives – now converted to 2-rail and fit them with RM motors.

Although I paid a number of visits to the Norris railway over a period of years, I never really got to know the man well. He was invariably a welcoming and a courteous host, and very willing to offer any help within his power to others who attempted to practise this hobby of model railways. Once he was convinced of a guest's genuine interest and involvement with the subject, further invitations would be forthcoming. Although he had the constant support and practical help of Bernard, as well as other skilled modellers, it was always he who was in charge; he knew what he wanted to accomplish and how to achieve his aims. His own expertise and skill plus considerable artistic ability enabled his plans to be realised in an amazingly short space of time. There was nothing arrogant in his attitude, nor did he make a parade of his wealth, and he took a genuine interest in the efforts of those who lacked his own facilities. He died before the completion of the railway, and it is fascinating to contemplate just what he could have achieved, had he lived long enough to see the completion of all his plans.

Bernard Miller was quite different from Stanley Norris in many ways, although they had in common this burning desire to work only to the very highest possible standards. There was something else which they shared – something far less tangible than mere high standards of workmanship, and far more difficult to define.

There was a breadth of vision in Norris's conception of a model railway which was not merely the result of an infinite capacity for taking pains. When you sat by the lineside, whichever direction you looked, there was an overwhelming impression of limitless space – as if the rails continued far beyond the confines of that building. The complementary genius in Miller was best summed up to me by a man who is one of the finest model builders of today – Vic Green. He had many of Miller's models through his workshop, and could recognise one of them almost blindfold. "Every one of Bernard Miller's models," he said to me, "had a soul. No-one but Miller could have fashioned them."

As a person, I found Bernard Miller the more approachable of the two men, and we met on occasions other than running sessions on the Norris Railway. He was one of those people to whom time seemed not to exist, and it is an abiding mystery to most of us just how he ever managed to fulfil his orders when he was in business. No matter what the circumstances, he would not be hurried, and I have known him take five years over the completion of a model.

Recently, Sir William McAlpine kindly allowed me to photograph a large collection of Miller-built models in his possession, and it has to be admitted that today there are many model-builders who are capable of producing work of equal – or even better – technical excellence. But to put the work which

both Norris and Miller did into true perspective it is necessary to view them against the model railway scene between 1930 and 1960, when so-called 'fine-scale' was the prerogative of the minority, and was still evoking some degree of hostile reaction amongst the people who modelled in Gauge 'O'. I have witnessed a dramatic shift of emphasis in this medium during the post-war years in that in 1954, the year the Guild was formed, probably not more than one in ten people worked in fine-scale, whereas today the proportion has swung very much in the opposite direction. I can well remember a group of enthusiastic modellers in 1954 discussing an article on Norris's layout which had appeared in a magazine. "We don't want any of this 'fine-scale' nonsense in the Guild. It is all very well for Norris with all his money, but the Guild is for *ordinary* people – not millionaires who can pay other people to do all the work for them." It is the measure of the members of the Gauge 'O' Guild that they quickly outgrew these infantile tantrums, and now regard fine-scale as the norm.

Pioneers are seldom popular people and prophets are not without honour save in their own country. But it is the Norrises and Millers of yesterday who paved the way for the standards of today.

GOG Slide collection No. 127

Victor Green

IT WAS NOT until 1981 when I first visited the late Colonel Hoare's magnificent Bromford and High Peak railway that I first heard the name of Vic Green. This is hardly surprising, as Vic is not one who seeks publicity, nor does he join model railway organisations, and it could be easily inferred from this attitude that he is some lofty recluse who does not care to mix with hoi poloi. When, later, I came to know Vic personally, and even stayed in his home, I found that nothing could be further from the truth. I suppose that my somewhat frivolous nature tends to attract me to people with a lively sense of humour, and this I found in full and overflowing measure in Vic Green. Within minutes of our first meeting we were laughing immoderately at the pompousness of some modellers, and my mental picture of Vic as a withdrawn and inaccessible person collapsed in ruins.

Life, however, is not all beer and skittles, so what manner of man is this who was respected by such people as Stanley Beeson, and patronised by those wealthy few who could afford his prices? In trying to answer this I must once again invoke the much-abused term of "Cheque-book modelling," and admit freely that there are very few people in this hobby who can afford to go to Vic Green for their models. Conversely, it would be impossible for anyone to work to Vic's standards unless these wealthy patrons existed.

Vic's father was an engine-driver, and hanging in his magnificently appointed workshop is a large photograph taken by Ken Leech of Vic's father standing on the platform at Chippenham station, about to mount his beautiful G.W.R. King footplate. It is hardly surprising then that Vic grew up with a great affection for railways, and was very soon building models of the engines he knew well. However, his remarkable talent for model construction led him into a far broader field of activity, and he was soon making models of every imaginable kind, from road-vehicles to delicate technical apparatus, and when he started to work for British Railways Board, he found himself designing and constructing life-size replicas of all manner of vehicles and equipment. He was even commissioned to build models in solid gold to be incorporated into a jewel-studded coffee table for some fabulously wealthy Eastern potentate. As Vic told me – "Well, he *was* wealthy until he got my bill!"

I have heard it said of Vic Green by someone who had never even examined a Vic Green model "His prices are a rip-off" in tones of disgust. At the time I stayed with Vic, he was just finishing a superb model of the Merchant Navy Pacific CLAN LINE, and he had kept a record of the hours he spent on this model. I worked it out that if he had charged *half* the rate of pay awarded to a garage mechanic, that model would have sold at something like £17,000. Before even cutting the first sheet of metal or turning the first wheel, he went to Eastleigh, spending days crawling over the prototype, making detailed sketches and taking meticulous measurements. This of course incurred travelling and hotel expenses, and during the course of construction of the model he went there again to double-check certain details. Such meticulous workmanship makes it impossible for Vic to work in the market-place; like the great classical composers who relied on royal patronage, Vic must subsist on a handful of very wealthy enthusiasts. He is constantly rejecting his own work, his restless seeking after perfection making it impossible for him to accept anything but his best. And his best is very good indeed.

Just one example epitomises this attitude of his. He showed me a Great Western tender, with all the riveting detail. One of the vertical lines of rivets appeared at first sight to show all the rivets as being equidistant apart. Closer inspection revealed that two of these 'rivets' were not rivets at all, but bolts which held the tender's bulkhead. The little trays of bits and pieces which lay on the work-benches fascinated me, for they were all of such exquisite workmanship, yet when I enquired what they were for – these valve-motion brackets, headlamp brackets, cab-details – I was told that they were all rejects.

Suffering fools anything but gladly, Vic is scathing in his condemnation of many of the kits offered for sale at astronomic prices, yet he laughed happily when I ran my Leeds Model Co. litho Sentinel steam rail car, pointing out that it was a bit of model railway history.

"You, Jack," he once said to be in my back garden, "have something I have never owned – a complete working railway system. You paint the entire landscape while I do one tiny corner." Such is the generous spirit of this master-craftsman, but what he did not add was that my 'landscape' was the sort of print one could pick up in any junk-shop; his 'corner' is a detail from a Rembrandt.

This close up view of the wheels and motion of a 7mm Bulleid 4-6-2 under construction is worth careful scrutiny. No detail appears to have been overlooked.

As a craftsman, Vic Green is beyond the reach of most of us lesser mortals, nor would our more modest model railways be suitable for such superb models. We can but stand and admire. But as a person, I think he is best summed up by a friend of mine who is himself a gifted model-maker. He had just seen the Guild audio-visual programme I had made on Vic Green, and when it was finished he said:

"That programme should be compulsive viewing for everyone who calls himself a modeller. Before seeing it, had I met Vic at some exhibition I think I would have greeted him 'Good afternoon, Mr. Green.' Now, I think I would be more likely to say 'Hullo, Vic!'"

IN THE GARDEN
Martin Bloxsom

IF THERE is one thing you just do not do when in the company of Martin Bloxsom, it is doze off. He is a powerhouse of energy of sometimes almost frightening proportions, with a voracious appetite for work. If some project appeals to him, he will waste little time in allowing the idea to lie fallow; rather will he be up and at it!

Such people attract extreme reactions in their acquaintances and colleagues, which can vary between breathless admiration and envy to bitter resentment, the latter reaction being very common to those who prefer to sit back and criticise, but do very little else. If one is of the "something-ought-to be-done" persuasion, it can sometimes be intensely irritating to find oneself dragged into involuntary participation in doing that something. This is not to imply that Martin rushes headlong into a project without prior thought, although he may give that impression. The fact is that his brain works at such high speed that he can formulate a modus vivendi while you or I are still trying to perceive it.

Like so many of the friendships I enjoy today, I first met Martin Bloxsom at John Hart's house. At the time – that is, during the 1970s, I would stay at John's house from Monday to Friday when my work took me into Surrey and Kent, and Martin, who was teaching in Sussex – and was still a bachelor – would spend his weekends with John, enjoying both the railway and the help John would so readily give with modelling projects. Quite often our visits would overlap, and we would find ourselves together in that house.

There were a number of shared interests between the three of us – John, Martin, and myself – for we all preferred so-called coarse scale; we all had outdoor railways, and we all had a band of young helpers whom we trained in correct railway procedure, these lads coming from schools in our respective localities. However, it was not until Martin moved to a new home that he was able to organise his own garden layout, and he opted for stud contact, whereas John Hart's was outside third rail; mine still being clockwork.

It was difficult to keep pace with Martin, and it always seemed to me that when he found life becoming a trifle humdrum, he would rush off on a sabbatical and pick up a degree or diploma at some college, just to fill the lagging hours. Whatever Society or organisation he joined, he would quickly be elected to office, sometimes to the dismay of his brother officers, for they would find themselves suddenly galvanised into action by Martin's insatiable urge to get things done. So it was with the Guild, and quite often, where Martin was, there you would find a swarm of hornets buzzing angrily overhead. I often found myself opposed to Martin's extreme views, but it is a measure of the man that this has never at any time jeopardised our personal friendship, for what he does, he does with honesty of purpose and with good humour.

His railway occupies the entire length of his back garden, which is in the shape of a long, thin triangle, and it is clear to see Martin's predilection for the old Great Central Railway. Operational sessions usually see a number of young lads at the controls, and often there will be other visitors. It was in fact on such an occasion that I met the late R.E. Tustin, who lived nearby. Ray Tustin, the author of a definitive book on garden railways, was a greatly respected man in model railway circles, and was the draughtsman behind many fine drawings which have helped modellers over the years.

Martin's stud contact line – like John Hart's, was run according to timetable, and on correct block procedure in the days of steam, although he did have an emu of Watford (LMS) stock which ran on third rail collection.

I have had the pleasure of addressing the Lutterworth Railway Society on a number of occasions – once in the company of Ray Tustin, when he and I formed a sort of Brains Trust. (Ray was the brains – I was taken on trust).

The only time I have ever seen Martin completely subdued was the evening in June 1979 when we had arranged to meet at his home and go out to dinner together. Just before leaving my hotel to go and collect Martin, I had a phone call from home to tell me of John Hart's sudden death only a few hours earlier, and that was the news I greeted Martin with. It was a sombre evening, for we both had a great regard for John, and it was to him that we had always turned with our railway problems. To continue without him there was almost unthinkable.

Yet, as I have said elsewhere, to many of us John is still very much alive, for there is hardly a job on our model railways which we tackle without conscious awareness of John's teachings and example.

Martin is married now, and has inherited a step-daughter. I am not too sure what it must be like, being married to a human tornado, but one thing I am sure of – life can never be dull for his wife!

IN THE GARDEN

George Hinchcliffe

I T IS NOT always true that a man of enormous creative energy and skill is also a brilliant organiser; too often the reverse is true. George Hinchcliffe is both.

We first met at the inaugural meeting of the Guild in 1956, and up to the time of retirement, we met fairly frequently, for not only did we share a great hobby, but my work would sometimes take me to the school where George was Deputy Headmaster. In fact, my firm seemed a trifle surprised at the frequency of my visits to this rural educational establishment!

George will tell you that his earliest memory of being able to read was to recognise the name-board of a Great Central locomotive which passed close to his home; the engine was EARL BEATTY. During the 1939 war George, by then in the Royal Navy – encountered Robinson engines in many parts of the globe, including Australia, Algiers, and even Shanghai. After the war, George was the key figure in the creation of the famous Gainsborough Model Railway Society, which quickly gained official recognition locally as a youth project. Of this I have written more fully in another chapter, for what we are concerned with here is the railway (he hates the word 'layout', as I do, but it is difficult to avoid) in his retirement home. Fully to understand this, it is necessary to consider briefly the major events leading up to George's retirement.

Like so many active men, George was blessed with a wife who not so much stood behind him in all he did, but rather beside him. Where George was, there you would find Frances not far away, and this even extended to her taking up the post of School Secretary at the school where George taught. I so clearly remember sitting in her kitchen one day, shortly after the news of Alan Pegler buying 4472 FLYING SCOTSMAN from BR. Alan proposed to send the engine on a combined goodwill and business tour of the USA and he had invited George to go out as custodian of the engine. I asked Frances what she thought of the idea. She sighed.

"Oh Jack – if you could only have seen his face when he brought the news home – he was alight with excitement, and even if I had wanted to, I could not discourage him." That was Fran – her man saw something he wanted to do, so she would be there to support him.

The story of the disastrous USA trip and the consequent stranding of the engine in San Francisco, bogged down by enormous debts, and subsequently rescued by Sir William McAlpine, is too well known to require repetition here, but

George himself had given up a safe, pensioned professional career in teaching, and this must have caused him some dismay. Very soon Sir William formed an association with George by putting him in charge of Steamtown at Carnforth, a job which he tackled with all his usual verve and enthusiasm. Eventually – after 25 years' close association with his beloved FLYING SCOTSMAN – he retired.

As can well be imagined, retirement suggested no lean and slippered pantaloon to George; rather was it another exciting adventure, with the opportunity at last to build his own dream railway. Tragically, soon after moving to their retirement home, Frances suddenly became ill, and within days, died, so she never saw the completed railway George built. George himself suffered serious health problems, but faced these as he faced all things – a problem to be faced, assessed, and then coped with.

The new railway was an ambitious affair, calling upon all the reservoir of experience and skills which he had acquired over the different phases of his life. He had a large garden, and this he put to good use, building his railway at table-top height. An audacious conception in terms of sheer size, it incorporated a replica of the famous Glenfinnann viaduct on the Mallaig extension, and it was hardly surprising that Sir William McAlpine was invited to perform the opening ceremony, for it was one of his forebears who had built the prototype.

The civil engineering of the line was in itself a major under-taking and involved vast embankments of stone, but the entire project held overtones of George's irrepressibly puckish humour, which was always thinly masked by a deadpan expression. Calling upon his experience as a schoolmaster, he prepared a lengthy and rib-tickling document purporting to be a history of his railway – FORT FAY TO INVERCLIFFE. The story of the original survey was hilarious, and yet carried the air of authenticity. There were scurrilous references to connections with Crewchester, but these I am leaving in the hands of my legal advisers, Sue & Chansitt of Crewchester. The sketchmap of the original survey, perpetrated by one "A. Pratt" is full of Hinchcliffian humour, with gradients shown as "Up a bit", "Up a bit more" or "Down", followed by "Still down". Under the big viaduct lies a loch, and on a small island lies Dampwater Castle, inhabited by Colonel Dampwater and his mother, the Lady Blodwen. At the terminus in the train shed (you and I would call it a garage) one can see the head office of the FORT FAY FINE FRESH FISH FILLETING FACTORY (Prop. Fergus McFaherty and his brother, Findlay).

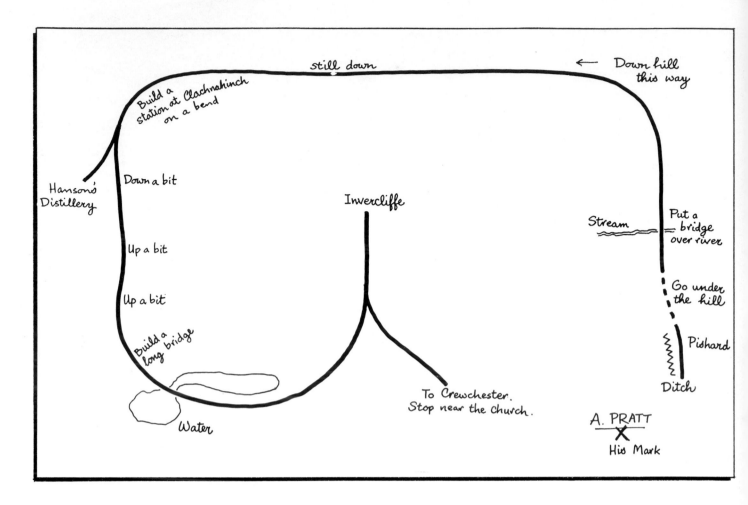

In the image (hand-drawn map):

still down

Down hill
this way

Build a
station at Clachnahinch
on a bend

Down a bit

Hanson's
Distillery

Up a bit

Up a bit

Build a
long bridge

Water

Invercliffe

To Crewchester.
Stop near the church.

Stream

Put a
bridge
over river

Go under
the hill

Pishard

Ditch

A. PRATT
X
His Mark

But be not deceived – the whole railway is run to a sequence time-table and in a thoroughly professional manner. Fort Fay lies on a silted up river estuary, where ancient, decaying barges may be seen lying on the mudflats. Great Central predominates, although it holds no monopoly, and some years back somebody drew George's attention to the fact that he had built models of almost every Robinson locomotive to last into LNER days. So George set to work to repair the omissions, and has now done the lot!

One day a few years back, George phoned me to say that Sir William was bringing his private train to East Anglia in order to experience what is left of the network of railways there, and I was invited to join them. It was a kind gesture, prompted by his awareness of our friendship, and it was quite an experience to travel in the luxury of a comfortable armchair which Bill placed on the verandah. A fine replica of that train had been built and ran on George's line, complete with Bill and his wife, in 7mm!

There is a most unusual feature on this railway of George's, and I can best describe it by quoting verbatim from the recorded commentary which we made to go with the slides. Up in one corner of the train shed is a closed-circuit TV screen, in which the operator can follow the progress of a train round at the other side of the house. Bear in mind that the period represented is the mid 1930s.

J.L.R.   What is that curious box stuck up on the wall, George?
G.D.H.   Ah now – that is interesting. Not long ago we met a bloke called Baird, and he had the most amazing idea. You know how it is possible to send sound waves – words in fact – without using wires?

J.L.R.   I know – it is called wireless.
G.D.H.   That's right! Now this geezer thinks he can send PICTURES in the same way. (Breaks into helpless giggles) Did you ever hear anything like it? I don't think it will ever catch on, but we thought we might give it a try.

In point of fact, the device is invaluable, for it is possible for the man in the train-shed to operate the entire railway, keeping the trains in view even when they are on the far side of the house.

It is difficult to assess the influence George has had on the hobby, especially in the field of youth activities, for generations of pupils have passed through his hands, both in school and in the Gainsborough Model Railway Society. My own debt to him is considerable, for he has done much for Crewchester, and we have a permanent reminder of him in the model of EDWARD THOMPSON, the A2/3 Pacific he built for us in 1957/8. After that trip in Bill McAlpine's train, George came up to my house, where I had prepared a train with EDWARD THOMPSON at the head. This, remember, was some 30 years after he had built the engine. We stood at the door of the garage in the gathering dusk, watching the train coming towards us. An enigmatic smile lay on George's face as he watched the train approach.

"Yes" he sighed. "Ugly beggar, isn't it!"

Only he didn't say 'beggar'!

Arrivals at Fort Fay on George Hinchcliffe's 7mm garden railway.

Ex NER 'Atlantic' crosses Clacknahinch viaduct.   Photograph – R.W. Swallow

Don Neale

IF YOUR only personal contact with Don Neale was to hear his voice, you could be forgiven for envisaging a slow-thinking, quiet man – someone perhaps associated with a comfortable armchair, a pipe, and glass of malt. The calm, almost drawling voice would go well with a good doctor, for it is always calm, relaxed and reassuring, but the plain fact is that Don was an officer in the Fire Service – hardly the sort of life followed by the 'lean and slippered pantaloon'! He is very much a man of action, although he does not outwardly display the dynamic energy of the man who always seems to be rushing all over the place doing things. Even today after knowing Don for 37 years, he is full of surprises for me. It is typical of him that in 1956 when Gauge 'O' seemed to be suffering an almost total trade eclipse, Don was one of that small handful of men who made the journey to London to attend that first tentative meeting of what was to become the Gauge 'O' Guild, his membership number being 9.

As I travel round the country making audio-visual programmes on every kind of model railway I am constantly encountering people who gratefully acknowledge the influence and inspiration of Don Neale's garden railway, especially those who have their railways out in the garden. Photographs of the magnificent stone viaduct which spans his garden have appeared in many magazines, and Don's authoritative book on Garden Railways has attracted the admiration and envy of many. But it was not until I first visited Don's house that I appreciated that the railway and the beautiful setting through which it ran is very much a team-effort of man and wife.

When Don and Joan married – many years ago – on their wedding day they had a photograph taken of Don's bride, standing on what looked like a ploughed field. It was that famous back garden! Very soon they were both at work, transforming the vision they saw then into the reality that is now, Joan being the gardener and Don the builder of the railway, although there must have been many occasions when their respective roles joined to work together on either garden or railway. A determination to work to the highest possible standards, each in their own specialised sphere of activity, has produced this quite remarkable end-product – a railway and garden which are fully integrated.

My first visit to Don was on the day of the wedding of Princess Di to the Prince of Wales, and the roads were empty as I made the not inconsiderable journey, for everyone seemed glued to their television. Not so Don, for he had been on duty all the previous night and had not seen his bed for some 36 hours. It was a fine sunny morning when I was led through the house and into the garden – a sight not easily to be forgotten, for the garden was full of colour. At the far end stood a row of coniferous trees, beyond which stretched the open countryside, but the eye was immediately held by that viaduct which stood like some miniature echo of Ribblesdale, lifting the railway across a wide valley of closely cropped green. For twenty years that massive structure had stood, in all weathers, and it bore the signs of its maturity. The years of warm sunshine were given back in the May brightness, and one had the feeling that surely this had stood for a century or more. In order to produce this effect, the ground had obviously been scooped out and piled high on either side, forming embankments upon which grew many shrubs, miniature trees, and bright blossom, through which the railway threaded its pleasant way.

The fictional locale of this railway had been aptly chosen, for it represented the Lake District in the days before that area of great natural beauty had become desecrated by motorways and its lonely fastnesses invaded by hordes of noisy cars.

The nerve-centre of the line, from which the entire system could be controlled was in a purpose-built shed, and in that shed lay two opposing termini, one in the form of a modest station, and the other a magazine capable of holding many trains. The station building was from the railway of the late Adrian Stedman, son of the famous Rex Stedman of LEEDS MODEL CO fame. Don had in fact built a link line between the two opposing termini, making possible a continuous run if required.

Where the line crossed the garden path close to the house, and at almost ground level, a lift-out bridge had been installed. At the far end of the garden, near the viaduct, Don showed me where there had once been a branch line, but vandals had broken into the garden and wrecked this picturesque feature; Don had not had the heart to try to rebuild it. There were various places and stations on the line which strongly evoked the Lakes – for instance Sawry Ferry on Lake Windermere.

I suppose there is a natural bond between people of similar interests, and this, coupled with Don's easy, relaxed manner and quiet friendliness caused the day to pass all too quickly for me, although I fear poor Don's eyelids must have been heavy by the time we had completed all the photography and recorded the

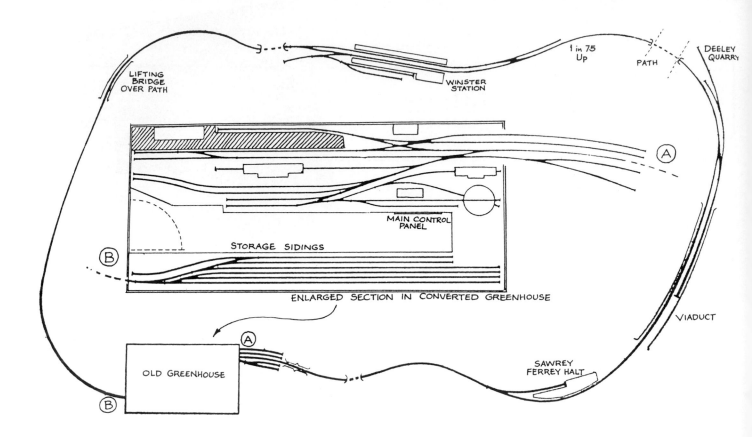

Labels in diagram: LIFTING BRIDGE OVER PATH · WINSTER STATION · 1 in 75 Up · PATH · DEELEY QUARRY · (A) · (B) · MAIN CONTROL PANEL · STORAGE SIDINGS · ENLARGED SECTION IN CONVERTED GREENHOUSE · VIADUCT · (A) · OLD GREENHOUSE · (B) · SAWREY FERREY HALT

commentary. I have been back there several times since that first visit, and Don has been to Crewchester, but the magic of that garden never fails to cast its spell. Like most railway modellers, Don is constantly introducing improvements and additions; he is never idle, yet he seems amazingly unaware of the reputation his railway enjoys among followers of the hobby. "My railway is right out of date" he claims "and has nothing of any real note in it." It is a pity he cannot hear what other modellers say about him when speaking to me!

I have related the anecdote elsewhere, but it does bear repetition. Just before I left Don on one of my more recent visits he asked, diffidently, "Would you like to see my party-piece?" Of course I would – and did!

The next ten minutes or so were occupied by Don fetching boxloads of wagons and coupling them together until he had a train reaching almost half way round the garden. Memory suggests that when I came to count them, there were 105 – but it was certainly in excess of a hundred. At the head of this prodigious train Don set two engines, and then turned his controller on. He runs on 24 volts, but even so the effect was remarkable, for that train wound its way slowly and surely round the garden, with never a wheel-slip.

"I'm only showing off," smiled Don, "We don't run this sort of thing every day, but it is a bit of fun, and rather satisfying." When the engines were uncoupled, Don invited me to grasp the leading wagon and pull the train. I was staggered – for it took all my strength to move that train of 100+ wagons.

Before I leave, on every occasion I visit Don's workshop where he always has a number of projects in hand – a new rake of LMS coaches – a new loco – new wagons – new trackwork and points.

Fireside – pipe – and glass of malt – there cannot be an awful lot of that sort of thing in Don's day, even though he is now retired.

Early in 1993 (the year in which this is being written) I paid yet another visit to Don – one which we had often discussed – when we wanted to go through the entire programme and its additions from time to time, weed out the less-than perfect photographs, add a few new ones, and make a completely new recording of the commentary. And that is one of the joys of working with Don – his quietly persistent demand for the best he can possibly achieve. Well, we did make that new programme, and it is now in circulation, an inspiration and encouragement to all who see it.

IN THE GARDEN
Jack Rothera

THE MANNER in which I made the acquaintance of Jack Rothera was, to say the least, unusual. It all started late one evening when the phone rang, and a distinctly northern voice greeted me with an apology for 'troubling' me at such a late hour, but that he felt he just had to let me know how he agreed with something I had written in one of the model railway magazines. I have described his voice as having a 'northern' intonation, but that is much too vague, for this was a voice clearly out of Yorkshire, a county I know and love well. Yet the call came from Lancashire – and is where Jack Rothera now lived. It is very doubtful if the name of Jack Rothera is known outside the immediate circle of his friends in Manchester, and perhaps his native Yorkshire, for Jack was no prolific writer on the subject of his garden railway "SCARBOROUGH TO ROSEDALE" and if he were alive today he would be utterly astonished to find himself within these pages, for his model railway was no outstanding example of the modeller's art, nor did his engines or rolling stock represent any striking or unusual prototype.

Yet Jack typified that vast multitude of people who build and enjoy their hobby quietly and unobtrusively, without feeling the urge to broadcast their modest accomplishments to the wide world. There was another reason why I find Jack memorable, and that was his infectious and effervescent enthusiasm, which bubbled from him in a torrent of sheer enjoyment. I will not insult Jack or his native county by attempting to translate into the printed word the rich brogue which so attracted me, but one could not long be in his company without sharing his exuberant enjoyment of just about everything.

Yet Jack had little to encourage this apparently care-free mein, for his wife was suffering the advanced stages of a terrible malady, calling for constant attention day and night. All this he seemed to take in his stride – his great spirit causing him to face the world with unquenchable delight, until quite suddenly, nature took its revenge and his heart gave up the struggle.

But for years, Jack would phone me at nights, when, I suspect he was on night duty at his factory and the calls were made at the firm's expense! During these exchanges, he spoke of his own garden railway, with many protestations that it 'were nowt much' and in November 1990 I travelled to Manchester to make a Guild programme on the Scarborough to Rosedale line.

The railway was a mixture of clockwork and electric, was built to coarse standards, and among the proprietary models was a liberal sprinkling of scratch-built items, notably a very passable model of a Cowan Sheldon breakdown train and crane. The Guild slide/cassette scheme was in its infancy in those days and I was ready to go just about anywhere, at any time to snap up another victim for the Collection, so the fact that the date chosen was 1st November did not deter me. Garden railways and November are not usually compatible! Yet on that morning in Manchester – not a city famous for its droughts – a wintery sun came through and the day, short though the hours of daylight were, allowed us ample time to complete our photography, although even this presented problems at first. Upon attempting to take the first picture, I suddenly became aware that the battery in my camera was defunct. Unable to leave his wife, Jack immediately supplied me with a guide in the form of a merry young teenager from next door, to show me where the shopping centre lay, and where I was fortunately able to obtain the necessary cell for my camera. This young man, named Graham, was also a keen model railway man himself and he showed me a diesel loco he had made himself at the age of twelve.

Jack was himself an ex-railway man, so his commentary was larded with knowledgable comments and enlightening sidelights on full-size practice, and he would often relate the scenes on his garden railway to incidents in his own experience on the railway. I found him full of surprises, not the least of which was a Bassett Lowke L.M.S. Compound which had a 25 volt AC motor which he drove on his 15 volt system DC. I did not even know that could be done but he did comment that the engine was not exactly a breaker of any speed records!

When we went into the house for lunch, I met Mrs. Rothera, then in the grip of Parkinson's disease, but she, too, seemed to make light of her terrible condition, and had somehow contrived to prepare a meal for me. During this lunch interval I noticed an electronic organ in the room, and nothing would satisfy Jack and his wife than that I should sit down and record for them a trifle I had composed for my daughter's birthday – to which the irrepressible Jack later added his own lyrics!

Back into the garden and another highly entertaining session with Jack and young Graham, until at last we completed the recorded commentary and I left for another address in Manchester where I was due to make yet another Guild programme. I bade farewell to this warm-hearted man whom, until that day I had never met, although our phone chats and correspondence gave me the impression that it was a reunion of old friends.

In order to write these chapters it has been necessary for me to dig out all the relevant Guild programmes, project them on to my screen and listen once again to the commentaries so as to refresh my memory, and I have to admit that as I saw that face and heard again the irrepressible fun in his voice, I found it hard indeed to accept that I would hear him no more. Earlier this year (1993) he phoned me – a long conversation, full of his spirit of fun and enjoyment, yet I was too obtuse to recognise that phone call for what it was. He dwelt on our long friendship, spoke of the pleasure my books and videos had given him, and how much he valued that friendship. I should have been able to realise that there was an undercurrent of finality about that phone call – that he was a sick man and was in fact saying "Farewell, old friend – it's been great!" A week or so later I heard of his passing.

I would add a footnote to this tale, and on a somewhat lighter note. When I returned home from that Manchester trip I went as usual to our Parish Church where I was sub-organist, and as I prepared the music for the morning service, the Vicar came into the church – himself a Yorkshireman. He knew where I had been, and as he passed the console he said, "Well, Jack – how did you get on? November for a garden railway is asking rather a lot isn't it?" I told him that despite the date of 1st November, in fact the sun had shone. Canon Kent grinned at me widely as he passed towards the vestry.

"Ah, Jack," he said, "God must be a Gauge 'O' man!"

Edgar Lewcock

The name of Eddie's Gauge 'O' garden railway is "The Butcombe Railway" with the sub-title of "Gauge 'O' in Gumboots" due to the fact that in wet weather, that portion of the garden which contained the railway, and was truly at the bottom of the garden, tended to become somewhat gooey with mud, for the garden sloped downwards. As I have a private line to the weather-man whereby in some 14 years I have never been rained off when I visit model railways, I never encountered this ooze; my problem when there was usually to find a spot of shade.

My first impression of the Butcombe Railway was that of coming home. Like my own Crewchester, Butcombe was built of sturdy coarse-standard rail, was at table-top height (oh blessed comfort!), was run on the ubiquitous 12 volt 2-rail system of current collection, and comprised both indoor and outdoor sections. Moreover, trains were offered from one section to another under the control of block-instruments and bell codes, a feature with which I am fully familiar.

A S OFTEN as not in those early days when I first knew Eddie Lewcock, my phone call would be answered by Mary, his wife, who would inform me – "No, Jack. He has just popped over to Mexico, and won't be back until Friday." Or it might be Venezuela or Timbuctu, or Winnipeg, or wherever, and it seemed to me that these trips on business were treated much as if he had just slipped down to the corner shop. How he ever found time to build a model railway is something of a mystery, but then the same could be said of so many railway modellers.

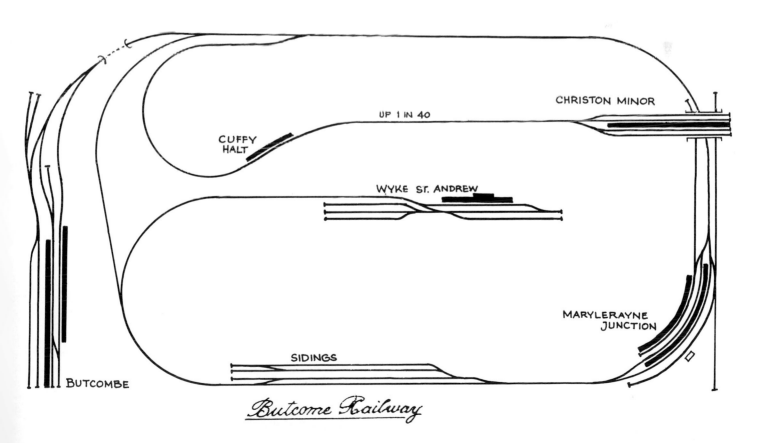

Butcombe Railway

Primarily inspired by the old Somerset and Dorset Railway, which is represented by two sets of coaches in that gorgeous blue livery, and two or three blue locomotives, the line also sees trains from the LMS and even the occasional LNER set as well as the almost statutory SR types. And – let it be whispered – the GWR has been known to appear on this cosmopolitan system, for Tony Chubb, a fellow Gauge 'O' man who lives nearby is clearly addicted to Swindon. Invariably, when I visit Butcombe, or when Eddie pays return visits to Crewchester, Tony will be with him, and the three of us make up a familiar and congenial team when operating each other's layouts.

The nerve centre of the Butcombe Railway is in one of the two sheds which lie in that lower portion of the garden, and is known as Maryleraine, the spelling of which has been subject to some dispute, for the older maps and historical documents always spell it Marylaraine, the railway preferring the more commonly accepted and chauvinistic male version. Who the original Queen was is not certain, but as the town was named after Eddie's own wife, Mary, the question becomes somewhat academic. Other stations on the line reflect the names of Eddie's family, with Christon Manor and Wyke St Andrew among them. Butcombe

itself, which lies in a second shed at the far end of the line, is the most remote terminus from Maryleraine.

Like so many rural railways, the Butcombe line is single-track, and provides opportunities for some highly interesting operation. Basically, it is end-to-end, between Butcombe and Wyke St Andrew, or up the branch to Christon Manor, but even the most intensive service can easily be managed by a team of three operators. However, when Eddie is on his own, or when he wishes to test some train or locomotive, he is able to bypass Butcombe and thereby form a continuous circuit.

Eddie's interest in railways stretches far beyond that back garden, for he is not only a keen follower of continental railways, sometimes gaining footplate trips there, but is a member of that band of enthusiasts who drive regularly on the private 4ft 8½in railway of Sir William McAlpine, where I too have enjoyed footplate trips, brake-van rides, and even the air-conditioned luxury of an open coal truck!

On the occasion of one of my visits to the Butcombe Railway, I took with me my (then) newly delivered Midland 7ft compound, an event of some significance, for Eddie had worked on – and driven – these handsome machines when he was at Derby Works. At the head of a fine rake of Midland clerestories, No. 1032 made a brave picture on that fine summer day. For me, these engines have a special appeal, for I grew up beside the old Midland Railway at Hendon, where the compounds were our staple diet on the more important expresses. Eddie tells an amusing anecdote about one of the old Midland drivers who was enthusing over the compounds and their remarkable achievements to such an extent that he swore that there was no engine to beat them. Unable to resist a dig at this voluble gentleman, one of his listeners reminded him of the notorious 'small engine' obsession of the Midland, asking "If those engines were so adjectival wonderful, what did you do when the train was too heavy for them?"

"Why" said the old man – "you use TWO compounds!" Such blind, unreasoning faith and loyalty would be hard to find among today's railwayman, I suspect.

To my mind, Eddie Lewcock's Butcombe Railway epitomises some of the best qualities of this hobby, for it is no narrow, obsessional preoccupation, but rather part of a broad, tolerant, and informed outlook on the whole spectrum of railways, with always a keen eye open to what the other chap is doing. In fact, the other chaps are frequently seen at Butcombe, for it is a meeting place for all who are absorbed by model railways of any kind, size, or shape.

43

Harold Aitcheson

O N THE FACE of it, the inclusion of this old retired signalman in a collection of studies which includes many illustrious names may seem a trifle incongruous, for Harold never achieved or sought fame, nor was his Gauge 'O' garden railway of special note. Yet he typified a certain broad cross-section of people who follow this hobby without any aspiration to super-detail models or sophisticated methods of control. He was a railwayman through and through, and he loved his work – so much so that even in his leisure hours he would operate his models as a relaxation.

If I am to present a true picture of Harold, it is necessary to consider the age in which he grew up. I was taken to his house by my good friend, the Rev. Alan Cliff, and to men of Harold's generation, the Minister was a figure to be respected, and never addressed by his first name, save by family and close friends. To today's generation this may appear feudal, for the pendulum has swung to the opposite extreme, and it would not surprise me to see someone today, on being introduced to the Archbishop of Canterbury, slapping him jovially on the back and addressing him as Charlie!

Alan had arranged this visit of mine, and I have no idea of what he had told Harold about me, but the fact remains that when we met, he was extremely nervous, insisting on addressing me as 'sir'. When Alan had departed I managed to convince my host that my name was Jack, but it was only with a manifest effort that he managed to get his tongue round this name. I realised later that much of his nervousness stemmed from the coming ordeal of facing a microphone, and once again one has to appreciate that to my generation – more so to Harold's – we had never even heard the word until we were into our teens. And again – in an age when children in infants' schools are weaned on tape recorders and computers, this may seem incomprehensible. His dread of this exposure to the terrors of the microphone had been offset to some degree by the idea of his model railway being in some way preserved for prosperity – a prospect which appeared to afford him comfort.

The railway was an extensive affair, starting in the shed containing a model of St Helens (Lancs) – a station Harold had known well in his younger days, and the track was coarse scale with centre-third current collection. As was invariably the case with this mode of collection, the trains ran smoothly and faultlessly. The models themselves, while not of Beeson standard, were very acceptable representations of their prototypes, and I would have been very pleased to see some of them running on my own railway.

We moved along the layout, taking pictures and making notes for the recorded commentary, until after half an hour I was aware that Harold's shyness was fast disappearing, and quite suddenly he turned to me – almost in surprise – and smiled broadly.

"You know, Jack" he said "I'm ENJOYING this!"

It was a rewarding moment.

From then on it was easy, and on that warm, sunny day we enjoyed both the railway and each other's company – I especially, for Harold had many fascinating stories of his days in the signal boxes along the North Wales main line.

When all the photography was completed we went into the house for lunch, there to be joined by Harold's son, and as soon as the meal was over I set up the microphone over a table, mounting on a high boom so that it could be suspended over our heads, and therefore out of Harold's line of vision. I have to admit that the following thirty minutes were hard work, for the knowledge that his voice was being recorded seemed to demoralise the old man. I have often found that one way of combating this form of stage-fright is to contrive some humorous element, and get my victim laughing, so I pretended to stumble over my own words, producing a phrase (accidentally of course!) which would have had me banned from broadcasting for life. On playing this back, Harold forgot his nervousness in a fit of giggles, and, slowly coaxing him back to the commentary, he began to relax and was soon chatting naturally. My over-riding aim in these interviews is spontaneity – to make them sound like two people sharing the enjoyment of the hobby, and it is for this reason that I try – almost at all costs – to avoid a prepared script.

I shall not forget that day, nor the unassuming character of Harold Aitcheson. It is not a spectacular presentation, nor does the railway break any new boundaries in excellence, but it epitomises a facet of our hobby not always recognised by clubs and model railway societies – the man who quietly and contentedly just gets on with enjoying what he has. Truly the salt of the earth.

When I had completed the programme I sent a copy of it to Harold, and Alan Cliff told me that the old man was thrilled with it, and the thought that many others would be able to share his enjoyment, even after he had gone. A few weeks later a small packet arrived for me. In it were two shunter's poles, made for me by Harold – "a very small thank you," he said in his letter – "for making the programme on my railway." That simple gift gave me more pleasure than I can say, and now that Harold is no more with us, I still use those coupling hooks, and every time I do so, I see the old man – and remember a summer's day in 1989 – and a very likeable gentleman who loved railways.

incursion into the realm of passenger-carrying live steam, for which he was building an engine. However, on that particular day, as I progressed round the garden, squirting my camera at just about everything I saw, the weather relented and the sun came out, transforming the herbaceous border into a mass of colour and greenery. Even now, there were further surprises in store, for Mike appeared in the garden carrying what seemed to me like a radio-controller, and which in fact was just that. No model aircraft were forthcoming, and I watched as Mike and his small daughter sat themselves on a garden seat not far from the viaduct. Very soon a train appeared from the signal box railway room and came smoothly up the garden, being operated by Mike.

"So you have radio control in your engines, do you?" I asked, somewhat superfluously.

"Not really" explained Mike. "This thing controls my controller in the railway room – not the engines." It was then that I discovered that Mike was one of that breed of supermen who know what goes on inside a television set; he was by profession a TV engineer; no wonder the control of models presented no problems to him!

From the time we had first mooted the idea of making this Guild programme, Mike had protested that although the microphone held no technical terrors or mysteries for him, using one was a vastly different matter.

"I'm no good at talking, Jack" he pleaded "You'll have to help me."

Having found this resourceful man highly entertaining – not to say instructive – ever since I had first met him, I foresaw no real problems in getting him in front of the microphone, and indeed, when it came to the point, he produced a commentary packed with fascinating information and larded with that irrepressible humour which was never far from the surface. Listening to it, one is strongly aware of a man who is not only possessed perhaps of more knowledge and skill than is given to many of us, but derives enormous fun and pleasure from what he does.

I have – at the time of writing this – visited and photographed over 150 model railways, many of them in unusual circumstances, but high on the list of memories is that of sitting in the upper part of that signal box with Mike, Margaret, and little Christine, enjoying our lunch whilst looking out over the garden with its railway, and beyond to the meadows and trees which stretched as far as the eye could see.

IN THE GARDEN
Don Wilson

THE SCHOOL mini-bus drew up outside the house, disgorging an assortment of teen-age schoolboys on to the pavement, eventually to be marshalled and led into the drive where I waited to greet them. The teacher in charge was one Don Wilson, head of the science department at a Suffolk High School – a very pleasant, dark-haired character – who was clearly popular with his charges, and he had phoned earlier that year (the late 1960s) to make the appointment. At that time we were becoming accustomed to receiving parties of visitors to Crewchester, so a full team of operators was present to work the complex railway.

I wish that I could remember more details of that visit – the first of several – but the fact is that, apart from recalling the event among many others, I remember virtually nothing. It was not until ten years later that I heard again from Don, who phoned to ask if he might pay another visit to Crewchester, and reminding me of his earlier visits.

"I want to refresh my memory of your railway" he said, and when I enquired how many I could expect he told me there would be only himself and his wife. Then, almost as an afterthought, he added "Since I saw you last I have lost my sight" – much as if he were saying "I've lost my handkerchief!" It took me a few moments for the full import of this statement to sink in and appreciate all its implications, but at length I blurted out something like "But that is terrible, Don! Do you mean you have no sight at all?"

"That's right" replied the cheerful voice at the other end of the phone – "but don't worry – my wife, Angela, will drive me there. And I can see an awful lot with my hands, you know!"

He went on to tell me how, since his blindness, he had built himself a 00 model railway, but that he needed something more substantial and robust. It so happened that a great friend of mine was Headmaster of the Grammar School hard by Don's Secondary School; it was he who told me what had happened. Don had developed diabetes, and, with complete kidney failure was on a dyalysis machine for 12 hours, twice weekly. My informant went on to tell me that he had married Angela just before the last vestiges of sight had left him, and that she was proving a wonderful support to him, even to the extent of attending Addenbrooke's Hospital (where Don had to attend twice weekly – a return trip of some 140 miles) in order to learn how to operate the machine and insert the needles herself. This enabled them to have a machine installed in their house so that there was no need to make the long journey twice every week.

On the appointed day, Don and Angie arrived on the first of many such visits, and even this necessitated a 50 mile return trip. In fact, after that first visit, Don was made an honorary member of the Crewchester Model Railway Club, attending on most Saturdays during the summer.

Those few years which followed were salutory, for when one saw the problems faced by these two courageous people, it was impossible to grumble at our own relatively small problems. Very soon Don had 'seen' the entire railway, and learned it to such a degree that we could seat him by the block telegraph instrument box at Ravensmoor, and he would supervise all train movements, recognising the different tones of the block bells, and even the slightly varying sounds of the instrument needles as they pegged over. He would remember every arrival and departure, and at which of the 7 platforms, so that he carried in his head a complete picture of operations. Many a time I heard him asking one of the operators on the departure side of Ravensmoor "Has that 5.20 left for London yet? I have offered it." Sure enough, the operator, busy on some other job, had forgotten to despatch the train!

Meanwhile, Don, helped by pupils from his school, set about building his own garden railway, for which he started to acquire models from well-known model-builders; all of them LMS, for his line represented a fictional section of ex-LNWR railway, very much influenced by his familiarity with the North Wales line from Chester to Bangor, where he was at University. Angela would drive him to various places in that area, photographing items of interest to him. Of course he could not see these, but she could, and she would help by doing such jobs as lining out coaches, at which she soon became adept. The table-top baseboard he erected himself, with some help from his lads, and much of the track he laid.

It was perhaps a little unfortunate that one of Angela's hobbies was fish, for which two sizeable ponds were built in the garden. Don quickly learned just how many steps, and in which direction they had to be taken in order to avoid these aquatic hazards, but on one memorable occasion he miscalculated and measured his length among the lilies and goldfish. Later, he swore that his wife was far more concerned about possible damage to the lining of the pond than to himself!

It was quite a revelation to watch other people's reactions when they were introduced to Don Wilson, for quite apart from normal compassion for a blind man, they were quickly affected by his enormous zest and enthusiasm. Both John Hart and Arthur Dewar were introduced to him; both invited him and Angie to stay at their homes, which they did, and upon his return Don would give me a full account of just about every detail of the layouts he had 'seen'. When viewing a model, it would be set before him where he could reach it – front-end always to the left, and his fingers would wander over it until his face would light up with recognition, and he would identify the model. Very seldom was he stumped.

Perhaps the most memorable event was the day I took him to Solihul where the Guild were celebrating their 21st anniversary, so that pinpoints the year as 1977. We wandered from stand to stand, exhibitors at first slightly uncertain how to react to this blind man, but, acting on my suggestion, they handed Don various exhibits, and in no time an excited discussion would take place, more often than not, with the exhibitor completely forgetting Don's blindness, and drawing his attention to such details as colour! The highlight came when I introduced him to that doyen of live steam, Eddie Cook, and very soon Eddie was passing over models for Don to examine. As we left every stand, we were followed by glances of sheer wonder from not only the exhibitors, but people who were standing by, watching. At the dinner that night, everyone within earshot of Don was smiling and laughing at his cheerful enjoyment of every moment. When I cut up his meat and gave him details of where every item was (meat six o'clock, potatoes 9 o'clock, veg 12 o'clock, and sauce 3 o'clock) he needed no further help, his fork going unerringly to what he wanted, and many watched him in wonder and near-disbelief.

At midnight we set off on the three-hour drive home, where he kept Angie awake until dawn, excitedly telling her of all he had done and seen.

From time to time a new model would arrive at his house, and immediately he would ask his wife to drive him the 25 miles to Ipswich "so that I can show to Jack and see what he thinks of it." Did I think the colour was right? Was that chimney slightly off-centre? Weren't those buffers wrong for that period? And so on. One day I have to admit to an unworthy suspicion, for whilst showing me a new engine he complained that the sandboxes on the front splasher were too far back. Had he, I wondered, shown the model to some sighted person who had spotted this minuscule error, and was now trying to impress me? Angie assured me that I was the first person to see the model since it had arrived, and when I dug out a photograph of the prototype – he was proved right!

In the course of time Don and Angela moved to a new house, about which he was characteristically enthusiastic. His own dyalysis room, his own study and workshop, and plenty of room for a large garden railway, upon which he soon embarked.

One day the phone rang, and when I answered it, Don was at the other end, speaking from Addenbrooke's hospital. "Sorry I shan't be along on Saturday" he apologised. "My leg is playing up again and they are going to do something about it. See you soon!"

They did something about that leg. They took it off, and he never came out of the building alive.

In my lifetime I have met many blind people – blind piano-tuners, blind telephone exchange operators, blind organists, all of whom seem to have conquered what most of us would regard as the ultimate calamity. But I never met a blind man who spread so much cheerfulness among everyone he came into contact with, and who made us so aware of how trivial most of our problems are. He loved it when people forgot he was blind, and said something extremely embarrassing. He would roar with laughter, enjoying their discomfiture, and delighted that they had forgotten his blindness. My own prize gaffe was when one day we were running my own railway he asked me if I ever ran at night time. Quite unaware of what I was saying I replied "There are problems, Don. We have tried it, but you try coupling up a goods train when the flood-lights cast deep shadows between the wagons." I heard him chuckle.

"Jack – I do it all the time!"

GOG Slide collection No. 124

IN THE GARDEN

Graham Taylor

A S CHIEF Medical Officer of an internatonal airline, Dr. Taylor's work took him world-wide, so, when I received an invitation to go and photograph his Gauge 'O' model railway, I did wonder if it might turn out to be some exotic and remote system tucked away in somewhere like the Andes. In fact, the line proved to be very English, bearing the name "THE MIDLAND, SOUTH WESTERN, AND GREAT WESTERN RAILWAY", and if this suggested pre-grouping days, I was not to be disappointed.

The house was not all that easy to find, for it lay well off the beaten track in a heavily wooded area, and it did strike me, when Graham Taylor and I took a pre-breakfast walk through the grounds of his house, what a wonderful place for a naturalist! However, it was not to study the local fauna that I was the guest of Graham and his wife, and eventually I was led from the house to a shed which stood beyond the garage and well away from the house. In this shed lay the nerve-centre of the railway, the central operating space being flanked on either side by baseboard, being connected beyond the far end of the shed by a half-hoop of weatherproof trunking.

On the left lay a terminal station, whose building reminded me somewhat of the old GWR station building in Staines. This had been built by Graham himself, as indeed had all the scenery. A beautiful rake of crimson Midland coaches lay in one of the platforms, while beyond the station were the loco shed and goods yard. The main line entered a tunnel which took the line into that 180° curve outside, after passing an underslung signal bracket.

To the right of this line, between that and the other side of the layout Graham had built a picturesque diorama which included a copse of trees, through which could be seen a factory. As he had been modelling for over fifty years, it was hardly surprising that the factory contained an echo of the 1930s and of a character who had been a regular and popular broadcaster on the radio. In those far-off days the BBC was ruled with almost puritanical strictness by John Reith, who insisted on conduct which seems scarcely credible today. For instance, announcers who read the news in the evenings (unseen by the listeners of course) were obliged to wear dinner jackets! All broadcasters were required to speak in what was usually referred to as 'the Oxford accent' – a sort of cut-glass, very 'up-market' voice. Gillie Potter was the very archetype of

this genre, and spoke with the ultimate refinement of this speech-style (although I was informed that in fact this was his natural tone) and would introduce himself with the words "This is Gillie Potter speaking to you in English, from Hogsnorton" – and there would follow a somewhat sardonic resumé of the local happenings in that fictitious village. One could almost 'hear' the monocle through which he would be reading! So it was that I read on the walls of that factory the name HOGSNORTON RUBBER FACTORY.

When the line re-entered the shed it ran into another station where the most notable item was a fine set of L&SWR coaches in their pre-grouping livery, headed by a fine class X2 4-4-0 in the same company locomotive livery and built by Graham. The coaches – both the Midland and the L&SWR were the product of a fellow-member of Graham's local model railway club, and were greatly cherished by their owner. Also noticeable on that station was a very fine lattice footbridge, unusually painted white, which was explained to me by Graham who said that when he had applied the white undercoat it showed up the delicate work of the bridge so well that he left it as it was.

Outside the entrance to this shed the upward slope of the land was built up into concrete terraces along which ran a number of tracks eventually all leading to their several routes. The one we followed took us deep into the woods before curling round through 180° to arrive at Updown Junction station, which was situated in a most unusual structure. This I can best describe as resembling a roadside cafe such as one finds on lay-bys, and patronised by lorry drivers, except that when the shutter along the front was raised, the entire area was occupied by baseboard – there was no room inside for an operator. The operator at that section would take the place of the customer, but instead of a steaming urn and plate of hot dogs, he would be faced by his controller and the tracks and station.

The main line from here on took us not only deeper into the thickets of birches and rhododendron bushes – these having been thinned out to make walking there easy and pleasant – but over falling terrain, so that at the far end the railway was at shoulder height. A raised dais of timber runs along the length of the station there, and on the day I was there the spring sunlight filtered through the trees giving a delightfully dappled and unusual effect for a model railway such as I have never before encountered. On such occasions one tends to forget the other side of the picture, when in autumn the leaves must fall thick and fast over the tracks. But on this day the scene was one of sheer serenity and being far from the madding crowd – in fact one of those peaks of perfection possible with a garden railway.

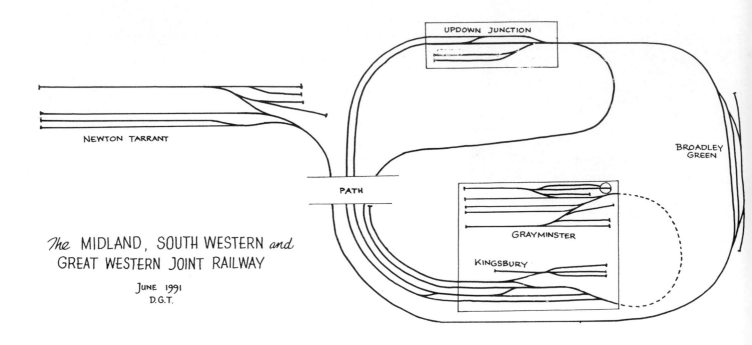

UPDOWN JUNCTION

NEWTON TARRANT

BROADLEY GREEN

PATH

GRAYMINSTER

KINGSBURY

The MIDLAND, SOUTH WESTERN *and*
GREAT WESTERN JOINT RAILWAY

JUNE 1991
D.G.T.

This station represented two phases of Graham's railway – the original stud-contact system, and the more recently adopted 2-rail method. From here on the line was 2-rail, and it was here that some fairly adroit wiring and change of control were found so that trains may continue under the later source of power supply. This later section took the line back through the thicket, this time on rising ground, to pass behind the railway room and on via those concrete terraces to a further terminus alongside the garage.

As I was conducted round this highly individual model railway by Graham Taylor, it was clear that he derived tremendous enjoyment and fulfilment from this relaxation from his exacting profession, and this is not always apparent with layout owners; some tend to make it an obsession which takes full control of their lives, leaving no time to sit back and enjoy the fruits of their labours, but always worrying about how the railway can be extended and improved. That is not to imply complacency in Graham Taylor, for there is always some project on the go – new coaches – a new locomotive – etc etc and I was shown into his workshop where he was currently working on some coaching stock.

The workshop itself was unusual in that it contained equipment not always associated with railway modelling, and I learned that Graham's wife produces exquisite jewellery, and shares the workshop.

"It solves many problems" Graham told me, "birthday presents are easy – a lathe or some such item without altogether altruistic motives! Also, that very tricky job of silver-soldering can be handed over to the expert. Marriages, we are told, are made in heaven, but surely they can be bonded in the workshop.

MODEL
RAILWAYS
AND THEIR
BUILDERS

Deryck Featherstone

GOG Slide collection No.35

THERE ARE certain names in the world of model railways which are inseparable from garden railways. Deryck Featherstone is one such and his instructive articles in various magazines must have helped many hundreds of aspiring modellers over the years, for he does not expect every one of his readers to be a chartered engineer, nor does he presuppose unlimited funds available to the modeller.

Deryck is a dyed-in-the-wool Great Eastern man, his own roots being in East Anglia, and his railway, although having its nerve-centre/workshop indoors, extends along the border of his long garden, and is built at table-top height. So far as I know, he has always worked to fine-scale standards, at least as long as I have known him, which is some 38 years.

Our long friendship has seen us meet in varying circumstances, often in mutual visits to each other's gardens; when I sought his help during my transition from clockwork to electric propulsion; as a user of the Guild audio-visual programmes, and in a totally different context – the school where Deryck taught, and which I sometimes visited in my professional capacity. Knowing of our friendship, the Headmaster would sometimes so arrange it that I lunched at the school with Deryck.

Deryck and his wife, Joyce, are two of the most hospitable people I have ever met, for their house and garden are almost constantly invaded by visitors. The annual open day in summer is an event I do my best not to miss, and the sun invariably shines on these occasions. Young and old throng the garden while Joyce and her helpers move round with plates of delicacies. But it is not all just for Gauge 'O' enthusiasts, for Deryck and Joyce will arrange days for physically handicapped people to come and enjoy the garden and railway. A recent innovation has been a 'live steam' day where the railway is handed over to locomotives with fire in their bellies.

The railway itself is built at table-top level and runs along one side of the garden, with a return loop at each end. At Bramley Junction (where once stood an apple tree) tracks lead off into an extension of the house containing a station called Wingham, complete with loco sheds, goods yard, carriage siding and transfer sidings to the Wingham Light Railway. This off-shoot from the main line climbs up until it passes over the throat of Wingham station, moving through 180° until it is hard against the opposite wall. Beyond the end of this, a track runs even further until it is directly at the rear of Deryck's workbench. By this route travel all engines or rolling stock due for service of some kind. The workshop section can be curtained off from the main part of the building so that in winter it can become a very snug, well heated workshop.

All the trains are of either Great Eastern or Midland & Great Northern stock, some of pre-grouping vintage, but mostly in LNER liveries. Whenever I visit the line I am reminded of Melton Constable in its heyday, with its assortment of coaching stock and locomotives ranging from ancient J15 0-6-0s to gleaming B12s and Clauds.

Deryck's modelling skills and enthusiasm have been handed down to succeeding generations of Featherstones, unto the third and fourth generations!

In all of us is a streak of residual childishness (otherwise we wouldn't play trains) but mine caused Joyce great amusement one day some years ago. When looking from her kitchen window she saw what she thought was a deformed man walking with a pronounced stoop and dangerous list to port, following the progress of a train at close quarters as it moved down the garden. Wondering whether she ought to render some form of first aid, she eventually realised that it was Jack Ray, his head about two inches from the engine, obtaining a highly convincing driver's eye-view from the engine. I might add that the effect of that distorted posture was quite astonishing, for with my left eye hard against the cab side, the impression of being on the footplate was quite startling!

I have never yet been to one of Deryck's Open Days when we have been rained off, and two explanations occur to one – 'The Devil looks after his own' – or – 'The sun shines upon the righteous'. Of the two, I prefer the second.

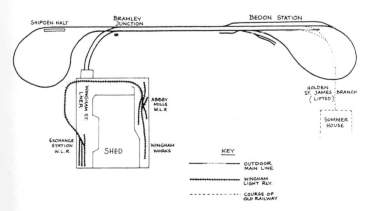

SHIPDEN HALT   BRAMLEY JUNCTION   BEDON STATION

WINGHAM ST LNER

ABBEY MILLS W.L.R

EXCHANGE STATION W.L.R.

SHED

WINGHAM WORKS

HOLDEN ST. JAMES BRANCH (LIFTED)

SUMMER HOUSE

KEY

—— OUTDOOR MAIN LINE

++++ WINGHAM LIGHT RLY.

----- COURSE OF OLD RAILWAY

Alan Brackenborough

I T WAS, I THINK, through Barrie Walls that I first became consciously aware of the name of Alan Brackenborough. I had been admiring Barrie's fine 7mm model of a Claud Hamilton 4-4-0, one of the two so-called 'royal' Clauds, which was painted in apple green, and I asked Barrie who had painted it.

"Alan Brackenborough" he told me. "But if you are thinking of getting him to paint anything of yours, I think you'll have a longish wait – he is a very popular and busy man." What I had in mind really was whether a Guild slide programme might be made on Alan Brackenborough's work. As time went by I met more and more people who had models painted by Alan, and the more I saw of his work, the more intrigued I became as to what kind of man did such fine work. Mind you, Alan would probably be the first to acknowledge that he was not unique, and that there were other equally skilled and gifted artists who painted models, but it just so happened that his name seemed to crop up in all sorts of places, so it was to him that I wrote, asking him if he might allow me to come and meet him with a view to making an audio-visual programme on his work; I had none such in my catalogue, and it seemed to me that people would be interested in a peep behind the scenes of a fine craftsman.

My letter to Alan brought a reply, saying that while he would be glad to allow me to come and photograph his work, his own garden railway was in a very early stage of completion, and might it not be better to leave my visit until something was running? Speaking to him on the phone gave me the impression of a rather shy man, and indeed Barrie confirmed that Alan was no back-slapping hail-fellow-well-met character, but a quiet and somewhat diffident man. He did however send me one or two photographs of a concrete multi-arch viaduct which he had completed, and these photographs showed me a quite remarkable scene. Of recent years, this sort of feature in garden railways is by no means rare, inspired no doubt by the superb structure in Don Neale's garden, but it was the setting which impressed me about these pictures. The viaduct was well-proportioned and made with care and skill, but behind it was a backdrop of a deep valley, beyond which lay a range of tree-girt hills, with houses here and there which, at that distance, seemed completely in scale. I was immediately reminded of Ken Payne's railway – when it was out-of-doors – breathtakingly beautiful as a backdrop to the railway.

Two or three years passed before I once again made contact with Alan, and a date in May 1992 was agreed. In fact, I arranged to spend a couple of days extra on my tour of Cornish layouts, as Alan's home lay only a short detour from my route to the West.

The day I set out was one of those perfect late spring days when the countryside was clothed in its fresh greenery, the sun pleasantly warm, and the blue skies dotted with high, fluffy clouds. Avoiding all motor-ways, I took a route which I had not travelled for over twenty years, along secondary roads which, to my delight, had altered not at all. When at last I found the village where Alan lived it was to step into a picture postcard world, with ancient stone-built houses set there long before the Town Planner had ever been thought of, a motley assortment of mellow time-weathered houses through which the village High Street struggled. And struggle it did, for the house where Alan lived gave directly on to the High Street at its narrowest point, with no room even for a footway, so that emerging from his front door was something one did with extreme caution. However, juggernaut lorries did not frequent this place, for it did not lie on a trunk route.

Alan's wife, Mary – who, to my great delight proved to be an accomplished musician – was recovering from a recent operation which deprived her of the use of one arm – and so I was lodged in a nearby guest house. That first day – or what was left of it – was spent in storing my photographic and recording gear in Alan's house as there was no room for prolonged parking anywhere near. Ken Payne drove over later that evening, bringing with him some work for Alan, and we sat out in that garden until well into the night.

In order to understand Alan's railway and the time I spent with him it is necessary to describe the place where it lay. The village High Street lay high on the side of a valley, the house being on the lower side, and, because of the terrain, while the house was at street level in front, by the time one reached the rear it was at first-floor level, and to reach the ground it was necessary to negotiate a stairway. At the foot of this was a path leading steeply downward, not immediately into Ken's own garden, but beside a neighbour's garden. Beyond this was spread Alan's own garden, lying on this extensive area of falling ground. The path, leading ever downwards, crossed a small bridge under which the Gauge 'O' railway ran in a cutting, surrounded by a huge lush green lawn. From here the magnificent prospect showed what had been only partially pictured in Alan's photographs.

At the lower end of the large continuous circuit of single track the railway was running at waist-height, and it was here that the viaduct stood. Photographs can deceive, but in this case no deception had been practised, for reality called for no embellishment by clever photography. Beyond Alan's garden the ground continued to fall away until it reached the floor of the valley along which the main trunk road ran. It was then that the magnificent hills rose, providing the spectacular backdrop I have tried to describe.

However, I was here to do some work – not just revel in idyllic scenery – and for some hours Ken led me from one part of the railway to another until I had covered it all. At one point there lay a triangle of track, one leg leading into the main shed where work was well advanced on a sizeable terminus. On the other side of the garden was another shed which housed a number of storage roads which were reached from a junction with the main circuit. A simple, but highly effective sector plate enabled all roads to be reached without the necessity of a series of points.

Naturally, this 'O' Gauge railway afforded opportunities for me to photograph many examples of Alan's paintwork, but one stands out above all others. Much as I admired the beautiful finish, lining, and lettering on the locomotives and rolling stock, my attention was drawn to a conflat, for which Alan had built a container. Bolted to the side of the solebar was a rectangular steel plate on which was painted in italic characters instructions and handling details, etc. In full size it would have been a fiddling job, but in 7mm scale it was mind-boggling! Immediately, I jumped to the conclusion that this must have been done in large format and then photographed down – an old trick by modellers, but when I suggested this to Alan, he told me, rather diffidently, that he had done it direct on to the plate. "I have to admit" he said "it was one of the trickiest jobs I have ever done." When I asked him how he had wrought this minor miracle of signwriting, he said "With a size 00 sable brush." There was just no answer to that!

John Hobden

Norfolk

NO-ONE HAD TOLD me what to expect, not even Frank Roomes, with whom I had been staying over the previous night. All I knew was that this man, John Hobden, had a very nice Gauge 'O' model railway based on Midland & Great Northern as his prototype. Very nice, too, I thought as I drove from Frank's hospitable house after breakfast – I have not much in the way of M&GN in the Collection, and this would be a welcome addition. After half an hour's easy drive, and following a sketch-map furnished by Frank, I found the address – a long bungalow set in pleasantly rural surroundings. I was welcomed by the bearded John, and taken in to meet his wife who, like John, was also a school-teacher. I sat, enjoying a cup of coffee, blissfully unaware of the hazards which lay ahead of me, and in the fulness of time, John suggested that we repaired to the loft where the railway was housed, so we set off into the long passage which traversed the length of the bungalow. Turning right in through an open door, I found myself in the loo, and was about to inform John that 'I am all right, thank you, for the moment' when I spotted the ladder leading from the floor up into the roof. Now, I suffer from rather annoying back-trouble, and ladders are not my favourite way of scaling heights, but manfully, I laid down my camera, tripod, floodlamps, case of gubbins, script-pad, and followed John up to the top of the ladder. When I reached the top my heart sank, for the headroom between floor level and the shallow-pitched roof was, to put it mildly, limited. John himself, lithe and athletic, found no trouble at all in moving about in this restricted space, and even in my despair I had to admire the sheer enthusiasm of a man who so wanted a model railway as to resort to such cramped quarters.

It took only four trips up and down that ladder to fetch my equipment up. The problem when it was up was where to lay it down. Having lowered the trap-door I now found myself in an area which would have delighted the more evil-minded members of the Spanish Inquisition, for the only postures available to the human frame were sitting, or standing in a position resembling a rather obsequious serf before his lord. It took me a few minutes to recover my breath, my composure, and my senses, only to become aware of yet more problems. Stretching across the width of this shallow loft was a series of beams, under which a particularly agile eel would have little difficulty in crawling, and over which it would be necessary to tie oneself into a sort of double clove-hitch.

Succour, however was at hand. Even as I started to tell John that this was beyond my physical capability, there appeared upon the scene a small lad – one of John's offspring who, John informed me, would help in fetching and carrying my equipment. To this nimble lad the obstacles represented a sort of superb play-centre – an adventure playground – and he dived and swooped effortlessly among the rafters. I gritted my teeth, kidded my tortured spine that this was therapeutic exercise, and took a deep breath. Looking round me I became aware that I was seeing a most convincing representation of a railway I had known well, and upon which I had travelled in steam days – the Midland and Great Northern. That low viaduct across the river – that could have been the one spanning Forty-Foot Drain, and the splendid double-viaduct on the other side of the room – surely I knew that? I did, and had often passed it when working in that area. The tan-coloured Beyer-Peacock 4-4-0 was pure M&GN reminding me of the heyday of Melton Constable loco sheds. The scenery, too, was completely convincing, and anyone familiar with that area would have had no hesitation in recognising where he was. I abandoned the idea of telling John that the task was physically beyond me, for the railway was really worthy of an effort on my part, so, painfully slowly I began to assemble my tripod, camera, floods, etc, and under John's patient guidance, shooting commenced. By lunchtime my back was a mass of pain, and I thought of the audiences who would eventually view the programme, seated no doubt in comfortable chairs in a cosy room or hall – would they have the remotest idea of the conditions in which the programme had been made? A martyr's glow of self-sacrifice warmed my efforts and strengthened my resolve. Perhaps, had I known what was to follow lunch I might have weakened even at this late hour, but the warm hospitality of John and his wife lulled me into a feeling of having suffered for righteousness' sake, and I enjoyed my meal.

Lunch over and done with, I expected to return via the loo (what happened, I wondered, if the room was occupied when visitors to the loft were in transit?) but instead, John led me the full length of the long passage to his study.

"Now" he announced cheerfully "we come to the awkward part of the layout – it is rather difficult to get to."

Resisting an impulse to scream, I wondered if this were some awful joke. It was not.

Leading up from John's study was another ladder. Reaching the top of this I was just about able to bring my shoulders level with the floor of the loft, for above my head was a sort of false roof (in fact it was part of the baseboard of the railway). Before me, and to my left were blank walls, while to my right was a narrow opening about the height of a low table. John shouted encouragement from below.

"You sort of twist yourself round so that your back is towards that opening. Reach and pull yourself on your shoulders and back until you are lying full length –"

My response to these obscene directions would not add materially to this account, but suffice it to say that as I am 6ft tall, and the available space was a meagre four feet I experienced some difficulty in following John's instructions. I prefer to forget the ensuing ten minutes while I crammed myself, my equipment, AND John into a space some 5ft by 5ft. Normal breathing returned to me after less than five minutes, the agony in my back abated sufficiently for me to take a few shots from a position resembling that of a deformed toad.

If this account sounds like gross exaggeration or poetic licence, let me assure you that it is not. Let me also assure you that by now the railway had so got me under its spell that I would have endured far more to accomplish the completed programme. The whole scene was so real and everything on the line – tracks, signals, stations, scenery and the trains themselves transported me back to the pre-war days when I had travelled on the line.

The agony and the ecstacy were not over yet however for, having finished shooting in that area, John said "We now go to Cromer beach station."

There was no apparent route to any other part of the railway, for everywhere was bounded by backdrops to the line.

"Follow me" said John, and he dropped flat on to his belly and proceeded to crawl under a tangle of baseboards, wires and other impedimenta until he disappeared from view. When I was in the Infantry I was very good at that sort of thing, but somehow the knack seemed to have escaped me in the intervening forty years, but I managed to squirm my way through the maze, pushing before me the equipment, until I emerged into an area which would have provided ample space for a brace of lean cats, but allowed minimal movement (and breathing) for two people. I began to long for the wide open spaces of that first place near the two viaducts – until, painfully raising myself until I could peer over the top of the backdrop I saw Cromer Beach station, and all my pains and aches vanished.

It was beautiful!

I have known Cromer Beach station for over half a century, and although my memories do not quite go back to the Victorian era depicted in John's model, I do remember that imposing station, with its weather screen on the seaward side and its opulent 'carriage-folk' atmosphere. It was impossible to visualise the hundreds of hours' loving work which had gone into every brick-course, every individual roof-tile, the overall glass saw-tooth roof, the weather-screen. It was all there to the finest detail, and the tribulations of the day would have been justified just to see that station.

I will not pretend that I was not glad when the job was finished, and John and I got down to recording the commentary – a simple matter compared to what had gone before, especially with John's schoolmaster experience of making recordings.

The programme in its completed form does show signs of the difficulties in making it; some of the pictures would not bear exhibition at the Royal Photographic Society's show, but they do, I hope, give a reasonable account not only of a superb railway, but of a man so dedicated to the hobby that rather than forego his own layout, he built it in the only available place.

MODEL
RAILWAYS
AND THEIR
BUILDERS

Leslie Bellamy

East Anglia

IT WAS AN EVENING I shall never forget! I had been invited to address a model railway club some distance from home, had made the journey specifically at the club's invitation, confirmed by a scrawled letter from the secretary, but when I arrived I was totally ignored while the members socialised among themselves. Never before or since have I encountered such ill manners, and the only reason I mention it now is to throw into contrast the behaviour of that club (which, by the way, no longer exists) and my meeting there with Leslie Bellamy. He had come along as a visitor, and observing me sitting by a radiator, ignored by all and sundry for over an hour, came over to make my acquaintance. It was such a thoughtful action that I felt the otherwise disastrous evening had been far from wasted.

Leslie was obviously embarrassed by the way the club were behaving, but as he had no part in the arrangements he was powerless to do anything other than to offer his warm companionship. In no time at all we had exchanged invitations to visit each other's layouts, and I learned that he was a retired pharmacist. (I remembered his shops in the local town).

My first visit to his home was memorable, for Leslie Bellamy had created a railway which was quite unique in my experience, and upon which I later based one of the Guild audio-visual programmes. The whole thing was in a commodious loft, running the entire length of the large house, and the scene which met my eyes was quite amazing. It is difficult to know where to begin, for there was so much to take in, but let me start by describing the railway itself. As would be expected of a man who had spent some half-century in Gauge 'O', the track was coarse scale, with centre-third conductor rail, and a somewhat bewildering layout of tracks on two levels occupied a considerable proportion of the available space. Everything I saw reflected the work of a skilled craftsman, and the detail was hard to assimilate at first viewing. But the most striking – and at first bewildering – feature of the railway was the livery of most of the coaches, and some of the locomotives. A bright, royal blue predominated, the passenger vehicles carrying cream top half reminiscent of the old GWR coaching stock. All these beautifully painted coaches bore a crest embodying a kingfisher, the bird of ancient Greek mythology representing the word 'halcyon'; indeed, the railway had the title of THE HALCYON STATE RAILWAY. Further evidence of this unusual connection between a railway and Greek mythology lay in the Gresley A4 Pacific (in blue, naturally) named KINGFISHER, and yet another blue 4-6-0 Fowler locomotive, numbered 6100, but named CYEX. There were other engines and other rolling stock which carried the liveries of pre-nationalisation railway companies. It took a little while to adjust to this unique conception, but very soon I found myself completely fascinated by a Tolkein-like world, where I would not have been altogether surprised to encounter Bilbo Baggins, or even Gandalf!

The next feature to take my attention was the stations and their buildings, together with the surrounding streets of shops, every shop completely detailed down to tiny 7mm models of the commodities purveyed. Naturally there was a chemist's shop, a furniture shop, greengrocer, newsagent, – a host of tiny buildings upon which I could easily have made a full programme. It would take many pages to describe all this minutiae, but it is all in the pictures I took.

The landscape was dotted with all manner of houses, cottages, public-houses, streets of shops, every one of which Leslie had built from actual prototypes which he had photographed, measured, and even been invited inside to measure up the rooms. Returning home armed with all the requisite data, Leslie would set to work on a mockup of the proposed building in corrugated cardboard, sketching in details of windows, doors, half-timbering, etc, and this he would place in position, leaving it there for a few weeks before deciding whether it would harmonise with the whole. If satisfied, he would set to work on the model itself, working on this until the last possible detail had been incorporated. Perhaps the most striking building was the low-level terminus which he called St Lowe, where stood a beautiful replica of Ingatestone station on the old Great Eastern Railway – a red brick, ornate affair with tall Tudor chimneys and much tricky decorative detail. The glazing of the windows was a tour-de-force, for these were extremely complex. Umbrella ribs had been used for guttering – knitting needles for down pipes, and everything spoke of a mind which was a master of improvisation. Even the butcher's shop had a window full of joints, made by actually cutting up model cattle and sheep into authentic joints!

Having spent a truly memorable day on this railway fairyland, I sent off the films, eventually putting together the programme which for ten years circulated among Guild members. Leslie came to Crewchester on several occasions, and spoke of additions and improvements to the Halcyon State Railway, so I suggested that we prepare a more up-to-date version of the programme. This was duly arranged, and once more I climbed to that enormous loft and beheld the colourful scene. Many alterations had been made, and these I photographed, but there was one which took my breath away. By any standards the new station building at Fairford (which had been a terminus on the old railway) was impressive, and I am sure Leslie will forgive me when I mention that he was now well into his 80s, so what I saw was all the more remarkable. He had built a facsimile of Chelmsford station as it was in 1856. Once again, one was struck by the attention to every detail of architectural embellishment – and this called for extremely delicate workmanship.

I have touched only briefly on the Halcyon State Railway, for it is not my purpose in this book to encroach upon the domain of the magazine article; rather am I anxious to present the people who lie behind the models. This octogenarian shows little sign of his years, for although subject to all the aches and pains which come to annoy our old age, Leslie has the gift of indestructible and eternal youth; his eyes are not dim – nor is his natural force abated! Indeed the motto incorporated in the crest of the Halcyon State Railway epitomises Leslie himself – PAX ET TRANQUILI-TAS.

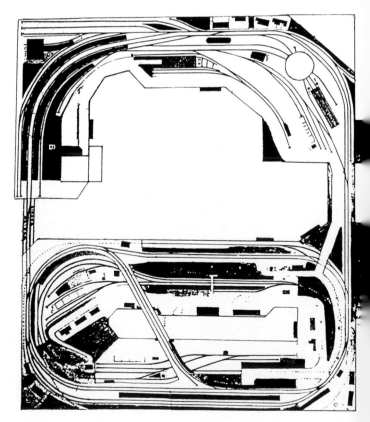

Jim Parker

The Lake District

I NEVER MET Jim Parker, and but for the prompt action of Bill Thomas (then editor of the Guild news sheet) and the timely help of Ken Ormrod, a most remarkable model railway would have been lost to posterity.

It all started with a phone call from Bill Thomas in mid-December 1989, when he asked me if I had ever heard of a man called Jim Parker. When I said that the name was unknown to me, Bill went on to say that he was hardly surprised, for Jim was a rather reserved and shy man who had come to the hobby only some eight years earlier, and had created '– one of the most beautiful model railways I have ever seen.' I have often heard this description applied to a railway which has impressed someone, and often I find that this 'most beautiful' railway is nothing out of the ordinary, for there are many fine model railways about today. However, coming from Bill, who has sufficient experience of layouts to be able to assess their relative merits, I sat up and took notice.

Jim Parker, according to Bill, was a motor car dealer in Kendal, with the agency for Porsche cars, and was himself a highly skilled engineer – hardly surprising in the circumstances! He had built this 7mm railway in a large loft in his home, but comparatively few people had seen it, mainly owing to Jim's rather retiring nature. It appeared that he had died a year previously, that the railway was about to be disposed of by his widow, but that she, although not specially interested in railways, was very anxious that some photographic record of Jim's work should be made. Tentative arrangements had been made for a local press photographer to come and take one or two photographs of the railway before it was dismantled, "But," said Bill "you know what press photographers are – they haven't a clue about taking a model railway picture. I wondered if you could suggest anything?"

It was a time for action, for Bill told me that our time was limited – Peggy Parker wanted the matter concluded soon after Christmas if possible, which gave us only weeks to act – with Christmas looming up to complicate matters. There was talk of at least part of the railway going to a museum in Barrow in Furness, but that sort of thing is fraught with problems for, no matter how altruistic the motives of the donor, museums, as a rule, do not have the space to accommodate these layouts, nor the staff to maintain them or work them. Stanley Norris was an example of this.

Bill was still on the phone, so I asked him whether Mrs Parker would agree to my invading her home for a whole day the following week, to which Bill replied "Get in touch with Ken Ormrod, who was a friend of Jim's and had been a close associate of the railway."

A phone call to Ken, who was a maths master at the local comprehensive school, resulted in a cordial invitation to stay with him, and that he would make the necessary arrangements with Mrs Parker. Within a matter of 24 hours Ken had been as good as his word, and he had arranged for me to go with him to the house where we would be able to spend the entire day making a Guild programme. So it was that four days later I set off on the 270 mile journey, only a week before Christmas, and in due course we drove over to the house where we were welcomed by Peggy Parker. She seemed very pleased that the railway was going to be fully documented in this way, for, as she said "Jim had very few visitors to the line, and it seems a shame that all his work should just vanish into thin air."

Ken Ormrod's help was invaluable, although he was far from being 100% fit at the time, and the exercise tired him considerably. What I saw when I arrived in that large loft fully justified Bill Thomas's enthusiastic description, for it was certainly one of the most beautiful model railways I had ever seen. The theme was the old Furness Railway line to Lakeside at the beginning of this century, and, like most visitors to the Lake District, I knew the area well, my memories of it going back well into steam days. But the section devoted to Lakeside station itself was breath-taking, for it represented the scene long before I was born, with the huge, ornate restaurant built above the quay. Enclosed in glass, with a

typically Victorian wealth of decoration and embellishment, a perfect scale model included the tiny tables, complete with white cloths, bentwood chairs, and plates, knives, forks and spoons all made to exact 7mm scale. The cutlery Jim had finished in white metal. Victorian ladies and gentlemen sat there enjoying the beautiful view up Lake Windermere as they took their refreshments.

Lying at the quayside was a fine model of one of the famous Windermere boats – this one being TERN. (Others were TEAL, SWAN, and I believe one other). What set the seal upon this scene was a most remarkable scenic effect. Jim had taken a photograph looking from the quay up towards Ambleside, had enlarged it up to the correct size, and fixed it as a back-drop so cleverly that it was very hard to see where baseboard and backdrop met. The effect was quite stunning, and anyone who has stood on that quay must surely recognise every detail – apart from the restaurant, which has long since gone from the scene. Another backdrop showed the hotel behind the station forecourt, perfectly scaled. The station building was a faithful replica of Lakeside building, and as if that were not enough, the layout of the track, signals, signal box etc were also there, correct down to the last detail – just as my old steam-day photographs show it.

It would take many pages in this book to describe the entire railway, but the sheer artistry and accuracy of it all fully justified Bill Thomas's description – it was beautiful. I spent some hours, ably assisted by Ken Ormrod, trying not to miss any detail, and of that there was sufficient for a hundred pictures. Further on the line reached Greenodd station – again fully detailed, and beyond that the line went on to cross the dangerous estuary of the River

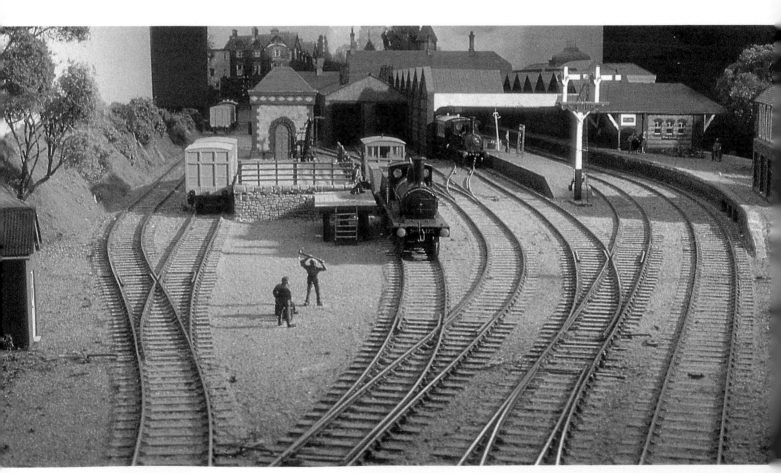

Leven by means of a plate-girder bridge, and once again Jim's brilliant photography provided a backdrop. No words of mine can convey the sheer artistry of that scene which, when photographed, made it difficult to distinguish from the real thing. Perhaps the effect is best summed up by a letter which came back from a club secretary who had borrowed three sets of Guild slides, including Jim Parker's. He says "We borrowed three programmes, but by common consent of all those present, we abandoned the other two, and watched Jim's programme through three times, to the accompaniment of many ah's and ooh's!"

After an hour or so I thought I had seen everything, but was yet to be shown another example of Jim Parker's resourcefulness. Ken told me that Jim was always fascinated by water, so when he built the model of the river running alongside the railway, he abandoned the usual method of sheet – or hammered glass, and used real water! This he did by boring a hole in the cistern, putting in a valve, and for running sessions, the river was for real! Incidentally it flowed out through an overflow just over Peggy's kitchen.

Although the railway represented the early 1900s, Jim was also interested in post-1939 war operation, so he acquired suitable locos and stock so that occasionally he could move forward in time.

I came away from that railway with mixed feelings; gratitude to Bill Thomas for letting me know about it (just in time!), and regret that I had not had more time to do full justice to the layout. In a few weeks at the most it would all be gone, and I wondered just what would happen to it. The tailpiece to the story is rather heartening.

As I had feared, the museum were unable to accommodate even part of the railway, let alone maintain it, but a very happy alternative was eventually found. The Haverthwaite and Lakeside Railway have built an enormous glass cabinet – sufficient to house the entire model station and its approaches, including the stunning model of the glass-roofed restaurant, and there it stands for all to admire, with an explanatory notice, together with a photograph of its creator, Jim Parker. What better place could be found, I wonder!

There was one very slightly discordant note which reached me in a letter from Peggy Parker, thanking me for the copy I had sent her of a magazine containing the photographs I had taken. Speaking of the exquisite model her husband had made of the Lakeland vessel, TERN, she told me that its appearance had been completely ruined by the addition of another deck, presumably so that another hundred or so passengers could be crammed on board – to the profit of the operators. But at least Jim's water-line model, detailed to the last degree, allows us to appreciate how that beautiful boat once looked – before the accountants laid hands upon her.

MODEL
RAILWAYS
AND THEIR
BUILDERS

Alan Payne

The Kyle Line

A
LAN PAYNE is the creator of a model railway called BRAEMORE, which leaves little doubt as to whereabouts in Britain it is supposed to lie. Contained in a fair-sized garage, the line is in the form of a continuous circuit, a formation which is almost statutory in such restricted space. Again, it is no great surprise to find that the line includes two through-stations, Braemore and Plockton, giving a further clue as to where Alan gained his inspiration. If the foregoing seems to suggest another run-of-the-mill Gauge 'O' layout, closer examination of the line reveals a highly individualistic approach by its creator, for here is no stereotyped affair, but a work of great beauty and artistry. This is hardly surprising when one wanders round Alan's house, where you will find numerous examples of his skill as a landscape painter, his speciality being woodland, trees, and other scenes painted from nature. Representational art is often sneered at by today's avant garde, but the impression I gained from Alan's paintings is that I would be well content to have any one of them hanging in my own lounge where they would be seen day after day – and still never lose their freshness.

This gifted man has brought his love of nature and his skill as a painter to his model railway, where the trains run against a backdrop which is quite breath-taking, for one can almost smell the peaty marshland, the wild heather, and hear the burns running through their courses. More impressive still is the distant scene – perhaps one of the most difficult and elusive effects to get on such a backcloth. The hills really seem to be a great distance from the railway, and those who know their Scotland, especially the western Highlands, would immediately recognise the terrain.

I have suggested a locale which inspired Alan to build his railway, but alongside this lay another source of inspiration, namely Arthur Dewar's superb Gauge 'O' Highland Railway. A regular visitor to Arthur, Alan saw there exactly what he wanted of a model railway, and he generously pays tribute to Arthur for helping him to see a mental picture of what he would do, albeit in a smaller area than Arthur had.

Braemore is clearly identifiable as Dingwall, the capital of Wester Ross, and the junction north of Inverness where the Wick/Thurso line diverges from the Kyle of Lochalsh line. Like Arthur Dewar, Alan places the period of his railway in the pre-grouping days in the first decade of this century, and all his locomotives and rolling stock are of this era. Braemore has a bay platform at each end, the southern one being used mainly for vans, and the northern bay for the little train to Strathpeffer. Had it not been for the obduracy of a local landowner, that is the route the main line to Kyle would have gone, instead of having to struggle up over Raven Rock.

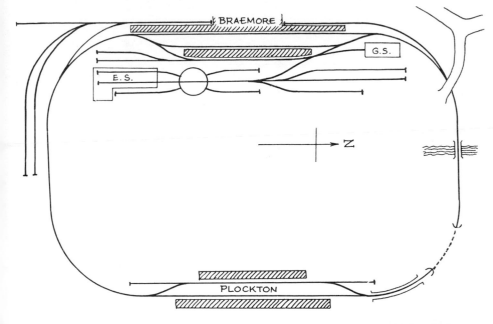

Although I have travelled frequently over this magical line in recent years behind diesel locomotives, Arthur Dewar can remember it in the days of steam, when Highland locomotives would battle their way up over those desolate, beautiful moors with their mixed trains — much to the disapproval of Westminster! The Highland Railway did not care overmuch for Westminster's autocratic rulings, and just got on with things in their own way. Watching the trains run on Alan Payne's railway, and relating it to one's own knowledge of the line, it is so easy to see just what things were like in those early days. The spartan comfort of the old Highland coaches and the hazards of Scottish extremes of winter would have made an adventure of journeys between Inverness and Kyle in those days.

If you have ever driven along beside that railway, parked on the shore of some loch, and wandered along the track, you are able to realise more fully the amazing civil engineering necessary to build this remote railway — far more dramatically than any impression you get from the comfort of a modern train.

And this is what Alan has captured so vividly. There is one scene in particular which fascinates me where the line spans a burn on the banks of which is a profusion of sedge-grass and other wild verdure, and on this coarse grass one can see tiny droplets of moisture glistening in the sunlight. Is it dew, or is it early frost which has just been liquified by the sun? The burn flows from a deep glen which runs back between the towering mountains, their peaks barely discerned in the mist, but although one could reach out and touch them in that garage, the eye insists that they are a day's march away. Such is Alan's artistry.

As Alan himself would readily admit, there are bigger and better railways than his, but I would insist that there are none to surpass the evocative beauty of his railway, and thanks to him we are able to recapture a bygone age in the story of railways.

MODEL
RAILWAYS
AND THEIR
BUILDERS

Richard Chadborn

Ambergate

IT TAKES QUITE exceptional moral courage to build a model railway which is supposed to represent a recognisable proto-type, for the moment you announce that your principal station is a model of Bloggsville Junction, you rouse that joyless band of know-alls who delight in pointing out that you have got it all wrong – that the station building was 72ft long and the model is clearly no more than 60ft in length. How they gloat, these armchair critics, relishing their own superior knowledge and delighting in proving the other man wrong! Far safer to hide behind the anonymity of a freelance locale, for then no-one may challenge you!

Richard Chadborn is made of sterner stuff, for he has taken as his prototype the old Midland Railway station at Ambergate, a subject packed with interest and railway history. My own memories of Ambergate are, to say the least, sketchy, for they are limited to occasional journeys to the north via Derby during the nineteen-fifties, when I would see just a part of Ambergate station perched high above the A6. I never had time to stop and explore this triangular junction, although sometimes I would see a Midland Compound standing at the head of a northbound train, or perhaps a Fowler 4F passing through with a goods train. For anyone interested in that part of the Midland Railway system Richard's garden railway is an education, for not only has be brought his considerable engineering skills to the making of the railway, but has researched his subject meticulously. He is a schoolmaster, teaching technical subjects, and so has access to sophisticated machining equipment which would be denied to most modellers, and this is reflected in (for example) the lattice footbridge spanning some of the platforms, made, Richard says – "from odds and ends of metal." Anyone who has ever attempted to build a footbridge, or even a signal post, of lattice, will appreciate this!

It may appear somewhat paradoxical to describe Richard Chadborn as a skilled engineer, and then in the same breath explain that the models he runs on the railway could hardly be described as showcase standard. Indeed, Bassett Lowke compounds run alongside a free-lance Duke of York 4-4-0, and quite happily so. In order to understand this apparent inconsistency, it is necessary to appreciate Richard's aims in building the railway.

Firstly comes his obvious affection for the Midland Railway in general, his chosen locale in particular, and the desire to operate a service such as would be in existence in LMS days. Hard on the heels of this preoccupation comes his wish to integrate the railway with the garden, making it a pleasant place to be regardless of whether one is interested in railways or not. Despite the fact that he has been living at the present address only a very short while he has already achieved considerable success in this direction. Then there is yet another consideration – he likes to have visitors to come and share the operation of the trains, including young boys (and their parents!), and to run Beeson-standard models in such circumstances would be to court disaster. As with any hobby, sentiment plays a part, for that Duke of York 4-4-0 was a gift from Richard's father when he passed his 11+ exam.

Emerging from a large outbuilding at the house end of the garden, the line runs northwards from Derby, past the site of the original station, and then into that triangular junction station, with the right-hand leg going off towards Chesterfield, and the left hand leg straight on to Manchester. The third leg forms a link between the Chesterfield line and the Manchester line. The platforms are all true-scale length, something which could be accomplished only out in the garden, but even here compromise has to be accepted, for gardens do have boundaries in the form of walls, fences, or hedges which will not be gainsaid.

As I have said, Ambergate station lies high above the A6 road, and even this feature is included in the model, the road being made from concrete and forming a sort of shelf upon which model traffic may run. The scope of this garden railway is the area contained between the Derwent viaduct to the south of the station to the Amber viaduct in the north. If one visits the area today there are still features which remain from Midland days; notably the two viaducts over the rivers, the two roads which pass under the railway, one being a lane leading past the Methodist church, and climbing steeply, while the other road passing under the railway is the Ripley road. Both these bridges have been faithfully modelled on the prototypes. The old hotel standing to the west of the A6 almost opposite the station, is still there, but the most striking section of the model is that contained within the triangle of the station. From this low level a long flight of wooden steps leads up to the central triangular platform where the booking office stands – again carefully copied from the original.

Such is his enthusiasm that Richard has been able to obtain some very rare prints of the railway in its early days, together with official diagrams and maps showing the precise siting of every signal and turnout.

When completed, this layout will present opportunities for a great variety of trains and routes. I came away from it with an infinitely clearer picture of what it was really like, and, linked with my very vague personal recollections of the place, and the vintage photographs Richard showed me, I felt as if Ambergate was a place I had known well all my life. Indeed, many of the trains which passed through Ambergate would have travelled past the bottom of our garden when I lived on the old Midland Railway in Hendon between 1921 and 1932, and upon which for five years I travelled daily to and from school.

MODEL
RAILWAYS
AND THEIR
BUILDERS

Chris Iveson

Strathclyde

ONE OF THE abiding mysteries of this hobby is the coy reluctance of the 'Modern Image Brigade' to come low enough to be shot at! They exist – I know that for I see articles in the model press from time to time – but the moment I contact them with a view to photographing them for the Guild, they run for cover. Time after time I have managed to contact club secretaries, tentative dates have been mutually agreed, and then ensues a deafening silence. This is so oddly at variance with my usual experience of model railway owners, clubs, etc, that I begin to suspect that there may be reasons for it. One possible explanation is that these worthy people who model in the contemporary railway scene are in some away unwilling to admit to such 'heretical' conduct, or fear that my own much publicised preference for steam may cause me to bring an unsympathetic attitude to my task of making a programme on their railways. In point of fact, exactly the opposite is the case, for my own lack of personal affection for modern image would cause me to take rather more care over such a layout. A good reporter is entirely impartial in his work.

In fourteen years of compiling this collection of slides, only two exclusively modern-image people have invited me to their railways – John Birch, and Chris Iveson. In the case of the former, I was not responsible for the photography, and therefore there would have been copyright problems, so Chris Iveson's invitation was doubly welcome!

The name of this layout was Fort Augustus, which, in view of the history of that ill-fated little line from Spean Bridge, seemed somewhat incongruous for a modern image railway. In fact, the railway turned out to be a most impressive representation of the railways in the Strathclyde area, the name Fort Augustus having no connection with Loch Ness.

If I approached this project with any sense of 'suffering for righteousness' sake' I was very quickly removed from that attitude, for I found myself becoming completely caught up in the infectious enthusiasm of its building. Unlike many who belong to a minority interest, Chris had no chip on his shoulder – no trace of the defensive belligerence sometimes found in such circumstances – but rather a broad outlook on the whole hobby. In fact, Chris revealed that his true roots lay in Somerset and Dorset, where he had in his younger days haunted Bath station. Furthermore, he hinted darkly that it was not impossible that he might one day return to this first love. At the moment, however, he was completely immersed in this fascinating Strathclyde system, a model railway with unusual features. To start with, it was permanently fixed in his living room, and in order to make room for my camera tripod and floodlights it became necessary to move the settee into the hearth! Even the house was unusual, for it lay – not by a road – but giving on to a greensward to which vehicular access was denied by a low brick wall, so that I did wonder about emergency services such as fire-engines and ambulances.

Modern image it certainly was, but, true to life, it still retained reminders of the older days, such as semaphore signals, and even a Great Northern style signal box – all, Chris explained, shortly to be replaced by telephone block-signalling. In the station yard stood a Wallace Arnold Tours coach, with left-hand drive, suggesting continental tours, while on a siding was a road-rail breakdown van, capable of moving to the scene of an accident by both road and rail. This van required a level-crossing in order to achieve the necessary wheel change to rail, but there is also (Chris informed me) a larger version which is able to make this metamorphosis by driving across the track at right angles, lowering a turntable and swinging into position with the flanged wheels now on the rails.

The 25,000 volts overhead catenary system is faithfully reproduced in the model, no doubt making track maintenance something of a problem at times.

One of the more worrying features of today's British Railways is the near-impossibility of keeping up with the flavour of the month – or to be more precise, the livery of the month. With the old familiar liveries now replaced by something resembling an explosion in a paint factory, it seems that BR are intent on sampling just about every known hue in ICI (Paint Division) catalogue, some of the results being colour combinations which set the teeth on edge! But Chris is not only on to their game – he is sometimes a jump ahead! If he gets wind of the fact that Strathclyde are going to change their colours to puce-and-off-cyclamen next month, his coaches appear in that livery weeks before the prototype appears.

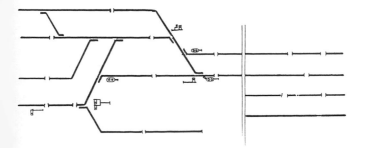

One of the great attractions of model railways in the days of my own youth was that one could identify with the real thing. As the steam age passed, so did this reassuring factor disappear, and now we have to rely more and more upon the fallible memories of old greybeards such as myself in deciding what it was all really like. But Chris has the inestimable advantage of being able to work from real-life. His assortment of contemporary ballast and hopper wagons is a delight to behold, with their curious names like Walrus, Whale, etc, and brake vans called Sharks.

One very impressive piece of work was shown on that railway – the conversion of the LIMA 'Big-big' coaches to a very fine model of a contemporary vehicle. This conversion included some very tricky work with a saw, for an extra window had to be added to each coach, to say nothing of the job of installing flush glazing. Chris also gets rid of the toy sliding doors, then, from a 'spare' coach he cuts a compartment and welds it into the new coach, bringing the latter up to scale length, and with 8 windows instead of the 7 in the original. Thus, from 8 'Big-big train' cars he is able to produce 7 scale-length cars.

Chris Iveson came over to me as a man with breadth of vision, considerable modelling skill, and an overall easy and tolerant attitude to the hobby as a whole. I had set out that day with a sense of 'duty' – that is, to leaven the steam-orientated Guild collection with some modern image, and was prepared to make an extra effort over something with which I thought I would have little sympathy. What happened was that I thoroughly enjoyed the day, photographing the railway, and Chris's company.

Keighley 7mm Group

IT WAS AT a Gauge 'O' Guild convention in Bletchley that I first saw Ravensbeck, and it was a case of love at first sight. Always having a weakness for model railways which exude atmosphere, this huge exhibition layout spoke clearly of North Eastern territory, and I edged my way, bit by bit, to the barrier where I could gain a clearer view of the quite mind-boggling amount of detail – far too much really to take in at one visit. One of the things I often read in letters which accompany the return of my audio-visual programmes is that the club, group, or even individuals who have seen them, often run the slides through several times, possibly omitting the commentary on second or even third showings, just so as to be able to linger on pictures of specific interest. This is just as it should be, for right from the outset I intended the recorded commentaries to be regarded as an optional extra. But when you first see a railway panorama of the size and complexity of Ravensbeck, the mind is unable to absorb it all at first sight.

From where I stood, just to my right was the centre-piece which gave the model its name – Ravensbeck station – a through station of such amazing detail that it was hard to know what to look at first! Those roads leading up to the station – surely those stone setts were all individually laid? That magnificent NE gantry just to my right was a little masterpiece, as was the stone road over-bridge just beyond it, and the very gentle left-hand curve of the tracks spoke of almost limitless distance beyond the bridge. The station-master's house, with its neat lawn, flower beds and greenhouse, the typical North-eastern footbridge spanning the tracks, the High Street with its houses and shops, dropping down from above rail-level to the low-level road – all were the result of countless hours of work by many dedicated people. The cemetery, later described by one of the operators as the dead centre of the village, was an unusual feature in a model railway, and this lay hard by the local golf club on the hillside which gave credence to the imposing tunnel-mouth which swallowed up the tracks. A stream running through the valley was spanned by a magnificent viaduct whose detailed structure could be a textbook for a bridge builder, so accurate was every part.

So absorbed was I by the wealth of detail that I barely noticed the trains! On the far side of the tracks beyond the station were a seriers of allotments, every one made by a member of the Group, and a row of cottages saw various examples of rural life, such as the woman sitting on her doorstep shelling peas, and further on, the smithy where a horse was being shod. Pages could be filled in describing the unending series of cameos which went to make up the scene, all of which seemed to cry out for my camera.

A notice-board proclaimed that the layout was the work of the Keighley 7mm Group, so, waiting until there was a lull in the procedure, I accosted one of the operators in the time-honoured way – "Take me to your leader!" – and I was introduced to Robin Taylor, whose response to my diffident enquiry as to whether it might be possible to include this magnificent exhibition railway in the Guild slide-cassette scheme was immediate and cordial. The railway, he told me, was to be open to the public in Keighley the following April on a Saturday, and that if I cared to come, they would extend the opening to include Sunday, that day to be a sort of 'private viewing' for me and my camera.

So it was that on the last day of April I arrived at one of the gigantic old woollen mills so typical of the industrial past of Yorkshire, and gave the agreed signal which would summon help in the form of two stalwarts of the club who each shouldered a share of my impediments and led the way up an unending series of wooden stairs to the floor occupied by the club. Half-expecting to find the Reverend Bronte paying a social call, I gazed round the huge area of uncluttered space where even Ravensbeck seemed dwarfed, and realised with some dismay that there was no way I was going to complete a programme in one day – there was just too much to be photographed. Such was the warmth of my welcome by this enthusiastic group that I immediately felt at home, and as soon as I had set up my equipment I realised that they had prepared for my coming by allotting a rota of two men at a time who would stand by to help, moving floodlights, tripods, and cables, crawling under awkward baseboards, lifting equipment over the tracks and in fact leaving me little to do other than just press the trigger of my camera. And when extraneous background, such as windows, lights, doorways intruded upon my viewfinder, a general call would go out for all hands to muster, a gigantic roll of cloth would be unfurled and held in position behind the scene I wanted to photograph, and held there by aching arms until the shot had been accomplished. Periodic coffee or tea lubricated the proceedings, aided by a stream of typical Yorkshire banter and good humour, so that the hours fled. Once Robin Taylor perceived that I was going to concentrate on every detail, regardless of how long it took, he went out of his way to make my way smooth, and we agreed that it would entail a second visit to record the commentary.

It was a photographer's dream-world, and I steadily moved round the layout, capturing every part of the scene and recording the details on my clip-board. When lunch time came, my hosts probably thinking that my weak southern stomach would be unequal to true Yorkshire diet, escorted me to a conventional

cafe, but when I assured that I was no stranger to Yorkshire, subsequent visits found us at the little pub on the street corner, consuming generous helpings of mushy peas and pie, washed down by a pint of Landlord ale. That evening I was taken to the famous Harry Ramsden's for the finest halibut steak I have tasted for years!

By the end of the long day I had taken well over one hundred photographs (three hundred in fact, for every shot was taken in triplicate). I had been shown how the pantile roofs had been made on the buildings — every one of which was taken from an authentic prototype — by encouraging the group to consume vast quantities of after-dinner mints; the crinkly packing making perfect pantiles. When I asked how they had achieved the realistic hay in the horse-drawn wain, silent fingers were pointed at Robin's beard. I was told, somewhat wryly, of the way a search had been made throughout the northern counties for a road over-bridge which would be suitable as a pattern for that bridge just beyond Ravensbeck station, only to find it ultimately hardly a stone's throw from their H.Q.

I returned home with many rolls of exposed film, sent them off for processing, and when they came back, sorted, labelled and made up the sequence ready for the addition of the commentary. Once more it was off to the North where Robin Taylor and two other members of the committee joined me at Robin's house, high up on the moors, and there we rigged the projector and screen, set up the microphones, and as the pictures were projected, shared the commentary, I merely acting as a sort of link-man asking silly questions. Four people joining in to make a commentary could well have been a recipe for disaster, with everyone talking at once, but in fact, such was the generous give-and-take atmosphere, that it all went as smoothly as a rehearsed script.

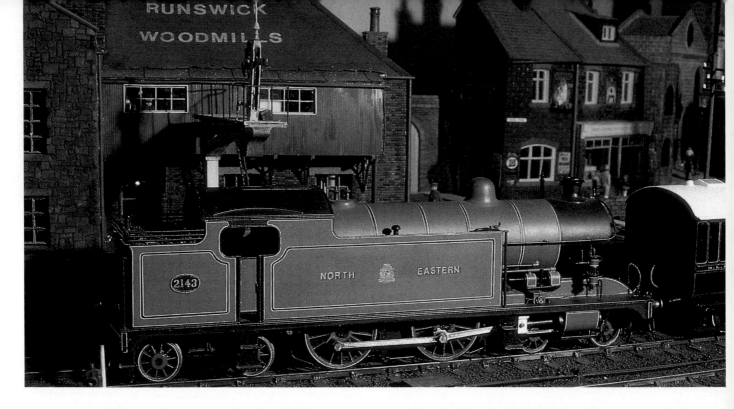

Not long after this, the layout was sold and the new RUNSWICK BAY layout was well advanced. It seemed impossible to me that this new layout could surpass Ravensbeck in excellence, but in fact, as is invariably the case, lessons had been learned from the old railway, and applied to the new, a smaller and more compact affair this time, but full of exquisite examples of modelling.

So once again I set off for 'pie-an'-mushy-pays' country, and made a Guild programme on Runswick Bay. Once again, I could fill many pages with descriptive detail, but as it can all be seen in the audio-visual programme I will content myself by saying that in Runswick Bay the viewer is transported back to the early days of this century, and to a river estuary (inspired by Kettleness, with more than a touch of Robin Hood's Bay), the actual mouth of the tidal river spanned by a viaduct of almost stupifying dimensions and detail. Once again I moved round the layout, aided by my willing helpers, photographing the beautiful details of the scenery. In fact, the scenery here takes precedence over the railway itself, and yet again, every building is one which can be found in prototype, with the exception of a few houses by the railway which have been contrived to fit in with the exigencies of contour and space, and even these look so authentic – so 'right' for their setting that one is convinced that these too have been copied from the real thing.

Seeing and photographing these two model railways has been inspirational, but even more important than the achievement is the heart-warming atmosphere in this close-knit group, the Keighley 7mm Group, and the merciless insistence that only the very best workmanship and artistry is acceptable.

When it came to photographing this group, another surprise was in store for me, for I was led through another vast warehouse on the same level as their club-room, sliding doors were dragged apart to reveal the balcony from which the sacks were winched to and from ground level. But it was the backdrop which these lads were after – the curving line of the Keighley and Worth Valley Railway. Typically, they had planned the timing of this picture to coincide with the passing of a train!

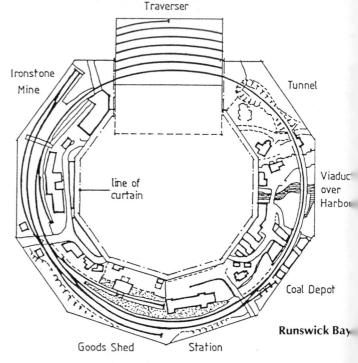

A footnote must be added. As I write, I have been told by Robin Taylor on the phone that Ravensbeck is back at Keighley again but that it will just not stand up to their present demands, so they are going to work on it to bring it up to what they consider 'exhibition standard'.

Yorkshire has long been a favourite county of mine – both the county and its people, for I have spent much of my working life there, and Robin Taylor will tell you quite solemnly that the main reason Jack Ray comes to Keighley is for "mushy-pays an' pie and a pint o' Landlord."

I can think of worse motives!

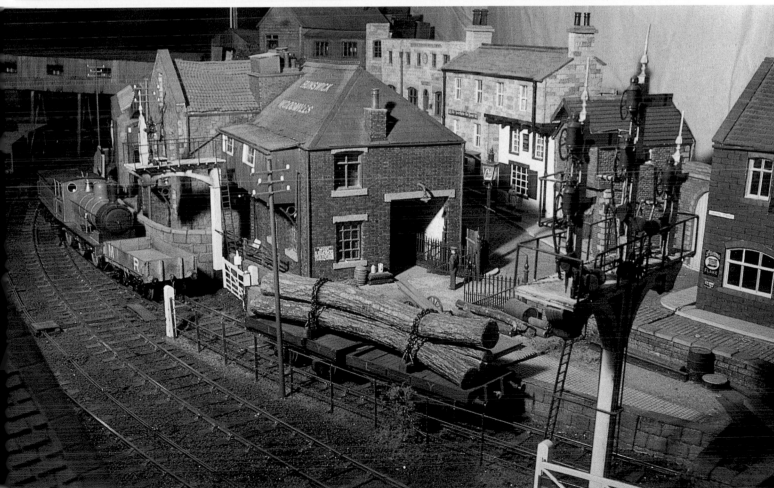

Renfrewshire M.R.C.

IN ATTEMPTING to write about a club or society, there is a great danger of omitting the names of key figures, whilst mentioning only those with whom one came into personal contact. Such might by the case with the Renfrewshire Model Railway Club, where I spent several extremely happy days, spread over two visits, and where I was made an honorary member.

The reason for my first visit in 1984 was to make a Guild slide programme on the club's Gauge 'O' layout named WALLNEUK. The reason for this name was that the main station on the line was based upon Paisley (Gilmour Street) station, at one end of which stood a signalbox named Wallneuk. The railway itself was quite remarkable, but what struck me most about this club was the air of organised and orderly effort. Wallneuk was one of several model railways there, in a variety of gauges, all housed in a pleasant building which the club actually owned, so they were not in the position of so many clubs who had to rent accommodation with the imminent risk of eviction. The big room which housed most of the layouts was well kept and in a fine state of decoration, and although inevitably there were places where building materials, paint, etc. had to be stored, here it was confined to unobtrusive places. Another unusual feature of this club was that they did their own catering – and this to a standard which would have done credit to a professional restaurant. At one luncheon where I was guest I was quite sure that there would be the usual band of members' ladies behind the scenes in the kitchen department, for the meal was beautifully cooked and prepared – but all by the members themselves.

It has occasionally been my sad experience (not, I am glad to say, in the field of Gauge 'O') to hear of clubs which confine their interests and activities exclusively to their own preferred gauge and standards, rigidly repudiating the merits of gauges other than their own. To these insular organisations membership, especially of the very young, is granted grudgingly, and often – so I am told by people who seek membership of the Guild – these clubs barely acknowledge the existence of newer members for years at a time. In contrast to this, the Renfrew people worked together for the common weal, so that if, for instance, the 00 people were staging an exhibition, people from the other gauges would abandon their own specific interest in order to help with preparations for the show. If I needed evidence of this it was provided when I set about making the programmes on the 7mm Wallneuk layout, for I was hardly allowed to lift or carry so much as a tripod or floodlamp. I had only to indicate the need for a flood to be held in a certain position, and willing hands leapt to my assistance. If some extraneous feature obtruded itself into my picture – a screen was produced and held in aching arms until such time as I had obtained my picture – and all the while the good-humoured banter was heard everywhere.

One of the irksome chores which accompanies the making of these programmes is the necessity to keep detailed notes of the content of every picture, for it will be many days before the processed films are returned, and I cannot just travel 500 miles to do the commentary. On this occasion, one of the members, Willie Pollock, volunteered to handle this job, and did it so effectively that when the time came to make the recorded commentary, everyone was able to read Willie's notes without any trouble.

Wallneuk is not merely a railway; it also includes a most impressive road system where trams run, and these fine models were the work of Nigel Macmillan, whom we shall meet on another page. The commentary was done by George Davidson and Nigel Macmillan, with a story-line linking the whole sequence of slides, starting with us boarding a tram upon which we were carried to the entrance of Wallneuk station. The road along which the tram travels is strongly reminiscent of that which runs beneath Gilmour Street station in Paisley, eventually rising to the high-level station entrance.

The railway itself is so devised as to make possible the running of almost every conceivable type of Gauge 'O' locomotive, from ancient Hornby engines with spoon collectors to superb fine-scale models such as are built by George Davidson – and others. There is such a wealth of lineside detail on this railway that the cameraman is almost spoilt for choice, for everything seen on our journey cried out for the close-up lens. So much was there in fact that I had to make a return trip to extend the original programme. This return visit to Scotland was made possible by several circumstances. Firstly, there were several other model railways awaiting my cameras, and secondly, the Renfrewshire MRC were so enthusiastic about the Wallneuk programme that they asked me – with some diffidence, if I would come again and make a programme on the 00 layout there, called THE DALHARCO COLLIERY LINE. They were prepared to meet all my expenses.

Here – yet again – I must express my gratitude to the Guild management in supporting my desire to include in the Guild collection of audio-visual programmes model railways in gauges other than 'O'. The Dalharco Colliery Line was indeed worthy of inclusion, for in its own chosen medium of 4mm = 1ft it was as remarkable as was the Wallneuk 'O' Gauge railway. The entire picture of mining was depicted here in minute detail, from colliery offices, pumping station, railway, with its complex exchange sidings to chemical works, iron foundry, and many other features. A village was modelled with shops, houses, hotel, and even a park where a military band was playing in the bandstand. Coal barges were to be seen on the canal, waiting beneath the coal drops which – like every other feature on the system, were actual working models. A great attraction at exhibitions, I was told, was the coal washing plant, known as 'the tippler', where a coal wagon

was lifted bodily from the track, hoisted to the top and tipped into the drum.

Another fascinating feature of this extensive layout – which occupied four sides of a large rectangle – was the series of reverse inclines which enabled trains of coal (or empties) to gain height.

Once again, as I moved my camera and lighting gear round, ready hands made my task almost a sinecure, and eventually I had covered every part of the layout. The commentary this time was recorded by the Chairman, Stan Kerr, and Treasurer, David Fowles, with a beautifully balanced mixture of southern English and Glasgow Scots accents.

I am sure that there must be times when the various factions in this club of mixed gauges find opinions differ and disagreements arise; the members would not be human if this were not so, but I came away both times with an overwhelming sense of a spirit of tolerance and mutual goodwill which pervaded this happy organisation. Certainly they showed great courtesy and cordiality to the stranger within their gates.

MODEL
RAILWAYS
AND THEIR
BUILDERS

Gainsborough M.R.S.

THE LONG and illustrious history of the Gainsborough Model Railway Society is so studded with personalities, all of great vision and tenacity of purpose, that it is impossible for me to attempt to describe them all, and even if I did so, I am bound to omit some key figure, thereby incurring the wrath of the rest of the team. Over the past 37 years I have been an infrequent visitor to the Gainsborough MRS, have been a guest at their annual dinner, have addressed them at meetings, and in a very modest way, shared some of the work of maintenance of the railway. My visits were rare simply by reason of the distance from my own home, but even that proved no obstacle to the Crewchester MRC making day-trips on the Open Days of the Society.

My personal friendship with George Hinchcliffe, their Chairman, gained me acceptance into the remarkable fellowship of the Society, and the infrequency of my visits seems to do nothing to diminish the welcome I receive when I do go there. Twice I have been there for the express purpose of making a Guild slide/cassette programme on this audacious model railway – a daunting undertaking if only by reason of its sheer size and complexity.

It all started when a few enthusiasts got together in 1946 to rent rooms in a large house in Gainsborough where they built the first layout, powered by clockwork locomotives, although centre-third pickup rail was soon installed. Public interest was quickly aroused, but the cramped conditions were unsuited to exhibitions, and anyway in 1949 the house was sold and the Society given notice to quit. It was then that a momentous step was taken, to utilise a large room in a disused school – the premises which are still in use to this day. By this time members were beginning to build their own models, and the centre-third rail gave way to outside third, still built to coarse standards. An exhibition, showing only scratch-built models, coincided with the 1951 Festival of Britain, and, encouraged by the success of this event, the more progressive members experimented with 2-rail fine-scale, not without misgivings from many members. However, the sceptics were quickly convinced, and in 1952 the first layout in this rather revolutionary medium was laid. It was an exciting and challenging time, with members all working on various models, all scratch-built, and mainly improvised from whatever raw materials were at hand, for there were virtually no manufacturers of parts, and kits were still far in the future.

Room by room, further space became available, until the entire building was occupied by the railway in a carefully planned system, albeit completely baffling to the visitor, who found it impossible to trace just what route the trains were pursuing! Originally rented from the owners, the Society finally purchased the premises, thereby becoming free of the threat of eviction.

Rare privileges such as this bring with them concomitant responsibilities which challenged the enterprise and tenacity of the officers, most of whom had been in it from the outset, and many of whom are still active there. There was no landlord to whom they could run, demanding repairs and maintenance; it was now all their responsibility and both manpower and money were a constant problem. A workshop and a canteen-cum-clubroom were installed, and later ladies' and gents' toilet facilities added, with all the work, including drainage, completed by members to the satisfaction of the authorities. New roofs and floors became necessary – it was a perpetual outflow of hard-won funds. To combat this, exhibitions were staged, the revenue from these enabling the ambitious aims of the Society to reach fruition.

In addition to all this, the committee had to build and maintain not only the railway itself – a gigantic system – but also organise the membership and foster the interest and enthusiasm of earlier days. Alan Pegler became the Society's President, his interest adding a spur – if spur were needed – to the remarkable progress of this railway. It was not until 1956 that I first visited the Society through the inauguration of the Gauge 'O' Guild, where George Hinchcliffe was the first Trade Liaison Officer and I the first Chairman.

My first impressions of the railway, apart from being completely overwhelmed by the sheer audacity of the railway's complexity and the high quality of the models, were of the quite impressive King's Cross room, as it is known. The model of King's Cross in 'O' Gauge, together with its approaches, including Gasworks tunnel (and in early days, York Road station and the line running down to the so-called 'widened lines' to Moorgate) occupied an area which most of us would consider adequate for an entire model railway layout. The great twin-roofs of the terminus were faithfully reproduced, as were the long platforms, the circulating area and the facade on the roadway at the front. To stoop down and peer through that entrance was to see King's Cross as it really was in steam days – long sets of Gresley coaches – the locomotives on Gasworks sidings – the old signalbox which has now gone from the end of the platforms – and the tunnels themselves.

If my schoolboy memories of visits to that station were stirred, later memories of the immediate post-war years were equally vividly evoked by the station at the far end of the line – Leeds Central, for on many a weekend I would park my car on the little slope outside that old station while I took the train home. That little slope is there in the model! I would not care to try to park my car in such a manner today!

Peterborough – Grantham – and several other stations were all

included in the layout; Hitchin, Hatfield, Hadley Wood – all these are there. Ferme Park – the huge goods depot at King's Cross is also modelled with its masses of freight wagons and vans, car-carrying train, and every other type of goods traffic. It demands a well-practised team to operate the railway, for just one bit of slack operation can bring the timetable to chaos.

The extramural activities of this Society are as enterprising as everything they do on the model railway itself. On several occasions they have produced important portable layouts for some important occasion. Coaching kits were produced and marketed by the Society. Special trains are chartered by the Society and of course 4472 FLYING SCOTSMAN has figured in some of these trips. The Society is recognised by the local authority as a Youth Group, and also recognised by the East Midlands Museum Advisory Service as a working museum. It is also a member of the Lincolnshire Museums Forum.

If I have omitted the names of the people who laid the foundations of this remarkable Society, and who – many of them – continue to run it, it is only because there are so many people involved – each in their own special role who have contributed to the making and maintaining of what must surely be one of the most impressive model railway organisations of all time. A notable feature of this band of enthusiasts is their total lack of complacency: they are constantly striving to improve the breed, and succeeding. It is this above all things which keeps alive the spark of enterprise which is so apparent when one visits the railway.

Long may it continue!

West Midlands

7, 10 & 16mm Group

THE ABILITY to make bricks without straw does not figure in my meagre list of accomplishments, and as I have never met him personally I am unable to present a personal account of Robert Head. If it is true of a man that "by his deeds shall ye know him" then I can tell you quite a lot about Robert Head, for on three occasions I have visited the West Midlands 7, 10 & 16mm Group's headquarters which are situated in and around Robert Head's house and grounds. On the occasion when I went to take official photographs for the Guild audio/visual scheme, my guide was Mike Thompson, who I am sad to report, died not long after that visit in 1987. From him, and from Roy Scott of The Sussex Model Centre, who is a friend of Robert Head's, I have been able to find a few facts about this remarkable man. He is a civil engineering contractor in a big way of business, including in his activities the building of motorways. One of the reasons why I have not had the pleasure of meeting Robert personally is that when I paid my first two visits to his home he was very seriously ill.

His large house is surrounded by a beautifully landscaped garden, dominated by a huge cedar tree in front of the house. Beyond this lies a thicket, and beyond that a sizeable lake over which he has thrown a superb replica in 10mm scale of Brunel's famous Saltash Viaduct over the Tamar. In order to carry out any repairs, maintenance, or rescue a stranded train, it is necessary to take a boat! But this striking feature is only one part of the panorama which confronts the eye when entering the garden, for the entire area is occupied by a breath-taking Gauge One model railway upon which a large assortment of live steam trains run. The main line is in the form of an extensive continuous circuit, with the double track disappearing into a clump of trees to the right of the garden. The end loop nearest the house stands upon slightly lower ground, and here the railway is carried on a series of red brick arches, the bricks themselves being slightly smaller than the standard house brick. At convenient places round this double-track circuit, stairways are provided giving access to the centre of the circuit. At the far side of the circuit a complicated series of tracks form a triangle leading to a large terminal station, with the steaming bay inside the triangle.

Left – Alan Gosling in charge of his radio controlled live steam locomotive.

Right – GCR 4-4-2 'Jersey Lily' in gauge one.

Below – G&SWR Manson 4-6-0 in gauge one.

From time to time Robert Head invites friends to visit the centre, and it was on one of those days that I first saw the railway, prior to photographing the whole thing officially for the Guild programme. It was a typical English spring day, with a cold wind and the rain coming down in a fine, drenching drizzle, but this seemed not to deter the enthusiasts, for the car-park was full and people thronged the lineside and the adjacent house and buildings. Beautiful pre-grouping trains ran round this Gauge One railway alongside modern-image diesels, all apparently unaffected by the weather. Curiously, when I once again visited the railway in 1994 the weather was even worse, the rain lashing down in torrents and making any serious attempts at running almost impossible.

The rain however was unable to affect the rest of this amazing place, for adjacent to the house Robert has erected a facsimile of a pub he once knews in his younger days – The Lame Dog – complete with pub sign, bar, and old-fashioned round tables with iron legs. Here one could restore the tissues and morale with all manner of food and drink while resting from the elements. This 'pub' was in fact part of a huge motorway contractors' building, and included a vast network of track in scales of 7 and 10mm to the foot, thus leading to the name of the centre.

Not only are there these three different gauges, but there is a section of dual-gauge track, including turnouts and even tandem points!

This adventurous Group was formed under the leadership of Norman Landon, its principal interest then being the running of live steam on 10mm scale track. Meetings would be held at members' houses, and occasionally hiring a church hall in which to stage exhibitions, until Robert Head, himself a member of the Gauge One Association, offered the Group permanent accommodation in this huge contractor's hut and the grounds of the house. This title of 7, 10 and 16mm may need amplification, so let me explain that the Group spread their interests and activities over three scales – 7mm, 10mm and 16mm to the foot. The 7mm track carries not only models in the same scale, but also narrow-gauge models built to a scale of 10mm or even 16mm to the foot. The Gauge One (10mm to the foot) tracks carry 10mm to the foot models.

benefit and demonstrated how he drove it by means of radio-control.

Although I was unable to meet Robert Head personally, I did see and admire some of the beautiful models he possesses in Gauge One, including a superb model of a Manson G&SWR 4-6-0 tender loco and glorious Jersey Lily in Great Central livery – surely one of the most beautiful designs ever to come from Robinson.

A rake of blue Somerset and Dorset coaches in Gauge One was taken out to the garden railway and run for me to photograph. Altogether, it was too much to take in even in three visits, and even as I write there is much work to be done on the indoor lines.

This very unusual model railway group, supported as it is in a very tangible way by the generous Robert Head, is not open to the public, although a form of 'open day' is held periodically by invitation only, and it reminds me of a remark made to me by the editor of the American magazine GARDEN RAILWAYS, Marc Horowitz, after I had taken him to Bressingham Gardens in Norfolk. He came away in a daze, and when I suggested that he had Disneyland in the States, he said: "Disneyland is commercial, noisy, and vulgar; Bressingham is one man's dream come true. We have nothing like it in America." The West Midlands Group may not be the consummation of one man's dream, for several people were involved in its beginnings, but it has undoubtedly gained both inspiration and support from Robert Head.

Included in the list of distinguished people who have been or still are associated with this complex collection of scales and gauges is Edwin Cooke, who was a regular visitor to the place, and ran many of his well-known live-steam models there. I also met Alan Gosling who fired his fine American Atlantic loco for my

Robert Scott

DOCTOR ROBERT SCOTT was one of those deceptive men whose image suggested a character totally at variance with the truth. His quiet, almost retiring manner, with his even quieter way of speaking, told nothing of the eventful life he had led; one time Medical Officer to the Doncaster Coal Mines, dealing with many dramatic and serious casualties in dangerous and difficult conditions underground, and later becoming Medical Officer of the North Sea Fishing fleet. Hardly a conventional G.P. with a cosy suburban or urban practice. He was one of the medical men who attended the terrible Harrow rail disaster, spending three days burrowing through that indescribable wreckage, rendering whatever aid he could. He told me that in all his medical career he had never seen such dreadful carnage, and that it still haunted his memory like some fantasy-nightmare.

Bob Scott is no longer with us, so it is possible to speak of where I met him, in the company of my friend Arthur Dewar, who had known him for many years. The Guild slide/cassette scheme was in its infancy then, and in fact this was to be only the seventh programme I had attempted. He lived in one of those elegant terraces of Victorian houses which typify the handsome town of Harrogate, and on the day we went there it was raining heavily. After the usual preliminary courtesies, we were led upstairs to the second floor, which, with the lofty, high-ceilinged rooms of those houses meant a considerable climb. Knowing that Bob had already suffered one heart-attack, I was not surprised to see a chair on each landing where, Bob told me, he was able to regain his breath, especially when coming up from the basement workshop.

It may well be that somewhere there is another model railway which is a working museum of the North-Eastern Railway, but if there is, I doubt if it contains so complete a collection of N.E. vehicles as I saw on that day. It had been his avowed aim to build a model of every N.E. goods wagon ever used by that Company, and he must have come close to realising that dream. In addition to the locomotives and rolling stock on his large Gauge 'O' layout, he had showcases full of obscure and ancient wagons, many with dumb buffers. All were built to high modelling standards, and it has to be emphasised that Bob Scott was well into his eighties when I met him, which meant that much of his earlier modelling life was in an age when almost everything had to be scratch-built; there were no kits available, nor was there the abundance of manufacturers of components which we enjoy today.

When, after we had completed the photographic session, and repaired to his study to make the commentary, Bob produced a script which he had written out in longhand on CARDBOARD – so that there would be no rustling papers to upset the microphone. When we did start the recording it soon became clear that there was going to be a problem with his age-weakened voice, and when later he sent me some additional slides (for he was an accomplished photographer himself) he sent also a full script, begging me to read it into the microphone on his behalf. I complied with his request, albeit reluctantly, for I prefer to let my audiences hear the voice of their host in these presentations.

Although there are notable exceptions, it is usually the case that a man's model railway reflects his age, for it is almost certain to be strongly influenced by the memories of his formative years, and it was quite clear to me from the outset that Dr. Robert Scott entertained an abiding affection for, and exhaustive knowledge of the North Eastern Railway. The time-scale of his railway was 1860 to 1922, which would embrace his own memories of the North Eastern and its constituent companies up to the time of the 1923 amalgamation of the 'Big Four'. It is not the purpose of these chapters to embark upon a detailed description of the railway, for the Guild programme already does that, but as the character of a man is closely interwoven with what he builds, it is interesting to consider the features of his model railway that set it apart from others, and remain fixed in the memory of those who were privileged to visit it. It was quite clear that Bob Scott preferred making models to running them, and in fact he openly admitted this to me. It was mainly at the instigation of a friend that he organised regular fortnightly operating sessions, occasionally bringing out from his show cabinets some of the historic vintage vehicles of such companies as the Stockton and Darlington Railway. Although his almost obsessive principal love was the North Eastern, nevertheless he liked to run trains or vehicles from other lines. The locale of his principal station, Newbrough, was an area south of York, and one of the important workings through here was the Aberdeen/Penzance train, with its complement of Great Western coaches. There was also a branch line which led off-stage to almost anywhere he fancied, and from this would appear Great Central, Hull & Barnsley, and many other 'foreigners'.

One notable feature of the Newbrough area was a ruined castle which stood high above the railway at the top of an embankment. It disguised – very cleverly – an ancient fireplace which protruded from the wall into the room. The resultant bulge in the terrain suggested strongly to him the motte of a castle, so he acquired a model castle populated by Crusaders and built it into the scene.

"I couldn't justify the presence of Crusaders" he told me "so I gave those to the little boy next door."

Dignity and impudence go hand in hand on this railway, and one of the first pictures I took was of a diminutive 0-4-0T standing beside the massive Raven Pacific.

Everything Bob built was meticulously researched and skilfully made, from the locomotives (most of which he had built himself), to the rolling stock, lineside scenery and effects, and buildings, every one of them clearly recognisable from its prototype. This naturally included the most recognisable feature of the North

Eastern – the distinctive footbridge to be found on every station. Built to a standard pattern, these bridges were always for double track, and if used on a single-track line, the steps would either be set right back against the fencing at the back of the platform, or even out in the forecourt or yard!

Bob Scott's lifelong love of the sea was clearly shown in a quay-side scene which was approached by a steep incline running down inside the main circle of a double track which occupied two rooms, and which was worked by a rail-car and one or two power-ful tank locomotives. The wealth of entirely credible detail reflected Bob's intimate knowledge of matters maritime, and the water-line models of vessels moored at the berths were all exact models of craft with which he was familiar. The backdrop depicted a large bay, upon which rode other recognisable sea-going craft.

One visit was entirely inadequate either to take in all the detail of this model railway, or to gain anything more than the briefest glimpse of the character of the man himself. He and his wife made us welcome without becoming effusive, and the overall impression I came away with was of a man of immense hidden reserves, and whom it would take a long time fully to know. Even after I left him that rainy day in 1980 he was building into his railway revised features. The engine sheds were dismantled and re-sited, offering easier access, and a new halt introduced on the branch line; the work of improving and maintaining the railway never stopped. We did try to arrange a further visit to update the programme, but the death of his wife, and other factors conspired to make this impracticable, so Bob, helped by friends who were also photographers, sent me further slides, including a fleet of period road vehicles which he had made, together with a script which he asked me to record for him. Nothing seemed to be too much trouble for this quiet man and he seemed genuinely pleased that his railway was going to be preserved for others to enjoy through the pictures and commentary. I do not know what happened to the railway after Bob's death in the late 1980s; probably it was broken up and sold piecemeal, but at least there remains a detailed record of a quite remarkable working museum of the North Eastern, and a monument to a man who knew and loved that railway.

If I have drawn a picture of a withdrawn, slightly aloof man, I have done Dr. Robert Scott an injustice, for although he was not a 'gushing' extrovert, his cordial and thoughtful cooperation with me throughout the making – and revision – of the programme on his railway was enthusiastic and heart-warming. Medical men are trained not to become emotionally involved with their patients for obvious reasons, and Bob obviously was influenced by this in his dealing with all people. But until he really got to know you, he had to be reasonably sure of what manner of person you were, and what were your motives. Once he was assured of my intention to make a permanent record of his railway, nothing was too much trouble. Typical of him was that script written out on cardboard; few people think of a detail like that!

Michael Lloyd

IF YOU HAVE TRAVELLED from Welshpool to Bala, almost certainly you will pass through the village of Llangynog, a pleasant village lying at the foot of the first really mountainous climb of the journey. Apart from the remains of a platform, little is left to suggest the picturesque little terminus of the Tanat Valley Line which made its way from a junction just south of Oswestry, through pleasant country until, meeting the huge bluff of the mountain, it gave up and called it a day at Llangynog. A modern wayside cafe with its inevitable craft centre attached now lies hard by the site of the erstwhile terminus, and modern houses now occupy what was the station precincts. It is possible to find many traces of the course of that pretty branch line if you explore the roads and byways, and as I often used to stop there for petrol, and enjoy a coffee on my way to Anglesey, I would wonder just what kind of trains once came here. I did trace the course of the Tanat Valley line in my gazetteer of pre-grouping railways, but somehow I never got down to serious investigation of the history of the line.

Then, a few years ago I heard of Mike Lloyd, a name being far from unknown as an authoritative writer on railway matters, and I discovered that he had used the Tanat Valley line as the prototype of his Gauge 'O' railway. I wrote to him and asked if I might come and make a Guild programme on his railway and immediately received a cordial invitation to visit him when next in the area where he lived.

It turned out to be a most interesting visit, for I was able to see exactly what that station at Llangynog was like in the heyday of its existence. When I say exactly, that is not quite true, for the exigencies of available space in the indoor section of the railway dictated a mirror-image of Llangynog station, every feature being reversed, yet still accurately represented as to detail. The beautifully made rolling stock and locos showed meticulous research of the prototypes, and Mike's knowledge of the history of the line was encyclopaedic. Even the great glowering mountain which hangs above the village was represented, and for several hours I took photographs and listened enthralled as Mike told me the reason for every item of coaching and goods stock, as well as the engines. He even explained how he made his own transfers!

The locomotives and rolling stock are almost exclusively of Cambrian origin, the period represented being the first decade of the present century, although there are one or two freight vehicles of 'foreign' companies, such as Great Western. All models are built by Mike himself, and comprise mainly 4 and 6 wheel passenger coaches.

Oswestry being the nearest market town of any size, the line would be used by inhabitants of Llangynog and all the other villages through which the line passed, so at holiday times many extra trains would be provided to take people to Oswestry where they could join the main network of railways to resorts. This would involve carrying much luggage, so Mike's trains often include both full brakes and brake-compos, the luggage compartment often being in the middle of the coach.

The indoor section could provide endless facilities for operating the model railway, but in fact, once the line reaches the garden it continues down the entire length of one side, running behind the flower-beds, along the bottom until it reaches an intermediate station, Hafod, where the single line becomes double, providing a passing place for trains. Beyond Hafod the line continues up the other side of the garden to the terminus at Machynlleth. Mike therefore has the best of both worlds – a self-contained indoor section for inclement weather, and the entire garden section to enjoy when conditions permit.

Having completed the photography, we went indoors to record the commentary, but here I encountered a most unusual problem. I had set up the recording gear, and after one or two 'practice' starts, I began the introduction, which follows a now-familiar pattern. "This is Jack Ray introducing another Guild slide programme, and the title-slide on your screen tells you that we are to see ––" and I broke off in mid sentence, for the headphones on which I was monitoring the recording were registering an enormous 50-cycle hum.

"Is there a freezer somewhere near this room?" I asked Mike, but he assured me that there was no electrical equipment anywhere near where we were working. Then enlightenment suddenly dawned on him. He led me out of the front door, and pointed. Between his house and the next stood one of those electricity sub-stations, and it was this which was causing the trouble. We therefore had to dismantle the microphones, cables etc, and seek an upstairs room as far removed from the source of the interference as possible, and there we managed to do our recording.

As I drove away I felt I had not only added a very unusual programme to the Collection, but had seen history come to life. Those fragments of railway cuttings, overgrown embankments, bridges, and derelict station buildings scattered along the Tanat Valley, now all had meaning for me, and I now knew what they looked like when those pretty little trains of 4 and 6 wheelers, and sundry freight trains once plied between Oswestry and Llangynog.

Alan Cliff

IF THERE IS one thing a long life has taught me, it is to give little credence to the archetypes presented by novellists and the film-makers. Take for instance, the parson, usually portrayed as a rather fragile, chinless character, much given to unctuous platitudes and benevolent inanities, and addicted to cucumber sandwiches and tea at church fêtes. Many parsons of my acquaintance are built like Rugby full-backs and could go four rounds with a heavyweight champion.

If the Reverend F. Alan Cliff does not quite fit this description, he comes pretty close to it, for he is a big man in every sense of the word. His energy – despite serious heart trouble – is such as to cause breathlessness in any who attempt to keep up with him as he strides through the town, so the imagination boggles at what he must have been like when blessed with full health! And lest an excess of brawn is to be equated with a compensating lightness of brain, let me set the record straight by mentioning in passing that Alan holds a Master's Degree at both Oxford and Cambridge Universities, to say nothing of various other academic distinctions.

Since his active ministry came to an end on medical grounds, Alan has had time to pursue more avidly his fascination by, and knowledge of railway and model railway matters. This preoccupation follows many paths, railway signalling being one, and on a number of occasions I have turned to Alan for guidance on signalling matters. He is a keen collector of vintage models, his study being a veritable museum of Gauge 'O' toys and models, including a small tinplate layout in full working order. The models themselves go back for a century – hence the title of the Guild programme "A Century of Gauge 'O'". He is the author of a monograph on ready-to-run 'O' Gauge locos and rolling stock – a therapeutic exercise recommended by his physician – and now out of print.

One of Alan's illustrious forebears was the founder of Locks of St. James – hatters of great distinction – and this has led Alan to christen his own Gauge 'O' layout "Lock's Sidings", upon which just about every conceivable model in that gauge – ancient and modern – may be seen. His collection of models is international, including manufacturers whose names are completely unknown to me, and all the time he is stretching out his exploratory enquiries to seek rare items. In order to make that Guild programme, we spent one entire morning photographing just about everything from tinplate crudities to scratch-built, fine-scale, super-detail models.

And here again I must explode a fallacy – that 'collectors' are a rummy breed of model enthusiasts who are willing to pay astronomic prices for hideous tin toys, provided that they are old, and have not been vandalised by weak-minded people who want to make them a little accurate and like the real thing. This type does exist to be sure, and if so much as a coupling varies from its original form, the fanatical collector will have a nervous breakdown.

To enjoy Alan's company is to understand why he was successful in his ministry at Central Hall, Edinburgh, and other demanding appointments, for the man just does not know how to spare himself. His enthusiasm in all he does – including his love of railways is infectious to a degree, and it is impossible to be with him for long without catching his sheer joie-de-vivre. Yet, while his hands will lovingly hold some rare vintage tinplate engine, giving the full history of its manufacturer, he will linger with equal devotion over a recently acquired scratch-built Claughton or Stanier 0-4-4T, commissioned from some notable model-maker.

In reading of the by no means uncommon predilection of parsons for railways, one is tempted to wonder if perhaps railways tend to take precedence over their vocation, but in the case of Alan this could never be said, for although he is no belligerent bible-thumping bore, and although he will never try to impose his firm faith on others, uninvited, one is left in no doubt whatsoever where his priorities lie, for they are rooted in solid rock. I think one of the nicest tributes I ever heard to Alan was from a strongly agnostic friend whom I introduced to Alan Cliff, and who in due course visited Alan in his home. His remark to me subsequently was "That man is so good, it hurts. Pity there are not more parsons like Alan Cliff!"

It is a continual source of mystery to me that comparatively few model railway enthusiasts take little or no interest in the history and evolution of model railways, for it is an absorbingly interesting field to explore. In the Guild audio-visual collection there are one or two programmes which concentrate on early models, especially such famous names as Hornby and Bassett-Lowke, but these are seldom requested. In apparent contradiction to this, one has only to attend one of the major model railway exhibitoins where there is a huge tinplate layout operating – and see the barriers packed with excited spectators of all ages. It would seem almost as if today's model railway builder is so obsessed with state-of-the-art hi-tech and meticulous attention to detail that he has little time for the days – not very long past – when these tinplate trains paved the way for what we now enjoy. Recently, at the Birmingham National Exhibition Centre, Bob Essery (the High Priest of Scale Seven) and I stood watching the vast tinplate panorama, where trains came and went without ever a derailment or failure of any kind – for hours on end, and Bob said, ruefully "We are both 'non-preferred,' Jack, for different reasons."

Alan Cliff, however, takes the broad view – demonstrating in a tangible way that there is room for all models – old and new. Despite his indifferent health, he is extremely involved in a wide variety of railway concerns, including the Bala Lake Railway, and the Joys of Life Centre in North Wales, and in all these different fields of activity he takes a practical and energetic interest. His own home, with Lock's Sidings, the tinplate layout, and the museum, together with a large library of railway books all speak of a man with a prodigious appetite for life, all aspects of which seem to absorb him, and I can assure readers that all this is but one part of an all-embracing interest in the world in which he lives and the souls of those to whom he ministers. A big man in every sense!

DOWN THE YEARS

Ian King

I T HAS BEEN commented elsewhere in this book that it would
be highly impertinent of me to attempt a character-study of a
man whom I had met on only one occasion, yet when I first
met Ian King in order to make a Guild programme on his model
railway, Grinling Junction, I felt as if I had known him for years. I
have also remarked before how the threads of friendship link the
many people I meet while making these programmes, and here
was yet another example, for I found that Ian had been a close
friend for thirty years of the late Geoff Bigmore (of Bigston fame).
I then discovered that Ian had worked in the Ministry of Defence
at Whitehall with yet another man whose railway I had visited and
photographed – Tim Taylor, whose Hartland Branch is featured in
the Guild Collection. Ian himself had retired from a post of
considerable responsibility at Whitehall.

It very soon became abundantly clear to me that Ian was
strongly drawn to what is sometimes referred to as 'the golden age
of railways', the Edwardian era before the First World War, and it
was to this period that he turned when planning his own railway.
Attracted though he was to the undoubted appeal of the country
branch lines with their picturesque little stations, he felt that such
a system would deny him the satisfaction of juxtaposing modest
little local trains with main-line expresses and long goods trains.
With (as he put it) expectation of no more than the normal life-
span, and with a growing family and a Building Society to support,
he embarked on a scheme which gave him the best of both worlds
– a main line junction station lying in the fictional town of
Grinling, between Doncaster in the south and Leeds in the north.
His branch line went from there to the felicitously-named Market
Gresley. The period was – not surprisingly – pre-1914.

But first, he had to cope with severe civil engineering problems,
for his back garden ran from the house in a gradually steepening
upward slope; hardly terrain upon which one might build a main
line. This he overcame by running his railway across the width of
the garden, following a contour line, and thereby achieving a fairly
constant mean height from the ground. However, such was the
slope that on one side the baseboard was almost at shoulder
height, whereas on the other side the ground quickly rose until it
was higher than the railway.

The outdoor section with a Leeds express composed of new Gresley bogies and an Ivatt 'Atlantic'.
Photo – Ian King

Reference to the diagram will show how the shed, which lay in the centre of this dog-bone formation, housed the nerve-centre of the railway and the junction station. To the south lay Doncaster, and the up and down lines through the station became a return loop with a crossing point provided in the bulbous end of the 'bone'. To the north things were a little different, for the entire loop was double track, the left-hand route leading to Leeds and the right-hand route going to Market Gresley. It seems that for a long time this little township of Market Gresley opposed the incursion of the railway, but in time it became only too clear that they were being bypassed by other towns, and seriously handicapped by lack of modern communications. They gave in at last and allowed the railway to enter their territory. To my mind, the name of Market Gresley has a curiously authentic ring to it, avoiding the use of 'joke' names (the 'joke' very soon wearing thin and eventually becoming merely irritating), yet conveying a very convincing – if imaginary – place.

Just as Geoff Bigmore made a backdrop of typical streets and buildings behind his Bigston station (Liverpool Street), so has Ian provided a backdrop for his Grinling Junction. There we see the Signal Inn and the Methodist chapel, but I was particularly intrigued by a large factory building across which appeared in large letters

S. A. Tanick Mills.

Great attention has been given to detail, such as rodding between signal box and points. It is always quite impossible in one visit fully to absorb every tiny, painstaking detail, and perhaps this is the beauty of slides, for one can sit and savour the features one missed at first glance.

Shortly after I had been to make that programme on Ian's railway I received a phone call from another modeller, himself a talented builder of coaches, and he said "I hear you have been to make a programme on Ian King's railway. I would like to borrow it, for he makes some of the finest Great Northern coaches I have ever seen."

When I come away from model railways such as Ian King's I wonder how many more such layouts exist where the owners prefer to hide their lights under bushels, and we never get to hear of them. This is a shame, although with today's lack of respect for other people's property, and vandalism rampant, one can hardly wonder at the reticence to publicise what is probably a lifetime's work, and risk wanton destruction at the hands of mindless people who take delight in destroying anything of beauty.

It is not the purpose of this volume to give detailed descriptions of model railways – that were better left to magazines and textbooks, but as a ham-fisted model-basher myself, I have to pay tribute to Ian's railway – not least of all to his really beautiful track-work, which I have described elsewhere as 'poetry in pointwork'.

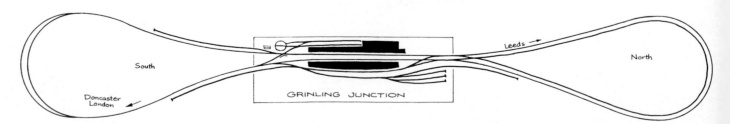

Barrie Walls

IT CAN HARDLY be said that my friendship with Barrie Walls started off on the right foot; indeed, everything seemed to conspire to give me a very wrong impression of the man before we actually met. Firstly, there was the matter of conflicting dates for Guild meetings. I would arrange a date for a meeting in Ipswich, and then find that this chap Walls had convened a similar meeting at the other end of the county on the same day. That was purely a matter of lack of good staff-work on my part, but the fact that it was probably my own fault did not tend to predispose me kindly towards this Mr. B. Walls. Bit of a thorn in the flesh was B. Walls, Esq. in my view. Then again I was influenced by the remarks of an acquaintance who, hearing me speak of Barrie, said "Oh – he's a shocking man! Browbeats his wife when she is operating the layout at exhibitions, in front of the public". Knowing my informant was given to rash sweeping statements I did not pay too much attention, but, you see, the points were piling up in my mind and I gained a rather unfavourable mental picture of the gentleman.

Anyone who knows Barrie and Rose Walls knows that a more united and happy team could not be imagined, and as Rose seems to know as much about running the railway as her husband, there is no 'browbeating' – quite the reverse, in fact.

Our first meeting took place in a rather unusual way. In 1981 I scrapped my 30-year-old clockwork railway and started to build a 2-rail 12v system. The main problem was that I could not afford to commission a whole new stud of locomotives, and anyway, of the 55 engines in the clockwork stud, I wanted to retain 12 of them, if only I could find someone to convert them. Not only was there the matter of cost, but at the age of 64, time was not unlimited. I had heard terrible tales of people being kept waiting ages for loco-motives they had ordered, and I did not really relish the prospect of waiting twelve years for my converted locomotives.

Whilst attending a model railway exhibition in Bury St. Edmunds I was discussing my problem with one of the exhibitors, who suggested "Have your tried Barrie Walls?" and when I asked him how I contacted Barrie he replied "By walking over there to the stand called WALLSEA. That is Barrie, wearing the woolly hat." And so it was that I first met the man who was to do much for my own railway, and with whom I have exchanged many visits over the past 12 years or so. The woolly hat, I learned later, had become something of a 'trade mark' and people had come to recognise him by it. (If anyone suspects that this headgear hides some deficiency of hair, I can assure them that Barrie has a head of hair which would be the envy of many a man half his age!). The result of this fortuitous meeting was that Barrie readily agreed to take on my clockwork engines, two at a time, building a new chassis with JH motors, 25/1 gears by Muffett, adding brake gear and cab detail. Within some 18 months he had fulfilled the entire commission, giving me a flying start on the new 2-rail system. Not only did this open up a new and valuable friendship, but was the start of many visits to each other's layouts.

And here I must touch on another facet of Barrie's character. His own models were of a far higher standard than mine, yet he never for one moment showed any less interest, or took less care in working on my rather cruder models than on his own detailed, fine-scale engines. One in particular I recall – a J3 0-6-0 tender loco by Ivatt, which had been built by the late Rev. Bernard Parley, circa 1935. It was over-scale, as were so many clockwork models of those days, in order to accommodate the spring-driven motors, and it was built for strength rather than delicacy. Barrie set to work on this historic monster with all the enthusiasm he brought to any job of work. Having been a shedmaster in steam days, he could work from memory, and often he would point out inaccuracies in blue-prints; he knew those engines from top to bottom, and could do much of the work from his own personal experience of supervising the maintenance of the prototypes.

It was a sad day when in 1992 Barrie announced that, owing to health problems, he was withdrawing from the exhibition circuit after showing WALLSEA MAIN at the Colchester show. Only those who have experience of taking a large Gauge 'O' railway to an exhibition can have any idea of what is involved, and he who aspires to convey Mohammed to the Mountain must be a very fit man himself!

One door closes – another opens! Instead of sitting back and bemoaning the passing of those hectic exhibition trips, involving hiring transport, and burning the midnight oil in assembling and dismantling the railway, to say nothing of long hours of operating, and anxiety about possible failures (rare, in Barrie's case, for his preparatory work was sound and thorough), Barrie started right away to adapt his railway to retirement.

One of the last surviving GNR Atlantics wearing BR livery and Barrie's outdoor section with concrete viaduct, colour light signals and fine scale trackwork.

Not now having to maintain a portable railway, Barrie set to work on radical re-designing of the indoor section, doing many of the things which were impossible before. Not content with this, he embarked on a long-considered outdoor section, planned years ago, but never having the time to realise it. This new section included a massive concrete viaduct of many arches, beyond which the line ran into a highly imaginative station – at present a terminus – but which I strongly suspect may one day become a through-station.

It is not my intention in these thumbnail sketches of the people behind the railways to encroach on the province of the magazine article, or even the Guild slide programme itself, by describing details of the layouts, but it is characteristic of Barrie's resourceful mind and skilful hands that he has already built into the modified indoor section a feature which I have never before seen in a scale as large as 7mm. This is a 'vertical magazine' which, in a very small lateral area, can accommodate a great number of trains. The extensive carriage sidings which occupied a large proportion of the railway room before could now be dispensed with and the space put to better use. For those who have not encountered the principle of the 'vertical magazine', it is perhaps best described as a robust structure based upon the roller towel, only instead of

flimsy towelling material, you have a 'towel' capable of carrying shelves on the inner surface. The roller-blackboard in classrooms could be used as another example of the concept. At one level, the two main lines pass across two of those 'shelves', which of course are locked securely into position, rather like the lock on a turntable. When a train is required to run 'off-stage' as it were, the 'roller blind' can be rotated, either lifting or lowering the shelf carrying the train, and bringing into phase either another train from another level, or just an unoccupied track. By careful organisation, the sequence of train movements can be maintained without resorting to spacious fiddle-yards or multi-sidings.

It is an almost childishly simple principle, but when one sees what robust and accurate workmanship is required to make this device work safely, one can only wonder at the audacious mind of this man. Woolly-hatted he may be – but woolly-headed never!

It would be less than fair to both Barrie and his son, Andrew, not to mention the way in which young Andrew has followed in the footsteps of his father. Andrew is the subject of another Guild slide programme, with his own compact UPWOLE exhibition layout, and this is still to be seen at exhibitions, often operated by Rose and Barrie Walls.

Fred Marshall

THE FURTHER you wade through these pages, the more you will find how the characters become interlinked. If John Donne had been a member of the Gauge 'O' Guild he would have been more than ever convinced that no man is an island, and Fred Marshall is a good example of how one acquaintance can lead to others, and each of the others lead in turn to more contacts.

It was very early in the Guild slide scheme that I travelled to a northern city to meet Fred Marshall, who, with his wife, Ann, had invited me to stay overnight. I had never even heard of Fred or his railway – "Bourne Bank and Wye Valley" until two weeks before I arrived at the large house where he lived, and at that time Fred was running a shop which specialised in philately, a subject on which he proved to be an expert. The extremely heavy lenses in his spectacles spoke of indifferent eyesight, and in fact I soon learned that Fred was suffering from a quite serious and uncomfortable problem with his sight.

From the moment I arrived it was clear that Fred was nervous about my visit, and later, Ann told me that for the past fortnight he had been desperately anxious that I would find his railway just not good enough for my cameras. His manner was nervous and almost shy, and he assured me that I would find no Norris-type fine-scale railway when we went to the loft. There was only one way to find out, and that was to go up and see it! Mounting the stairs we came to a landing from which a further flight took us to the large loft, where I saw the extensive railway spread out before me. It was, like my own, coarse scale, but it was packed with fascinating atmospheric detail, and I realised that here was a line which was going to invite many close-up shots. Something else struck me at the same time – the physical problems confronting the photographer, to say nothing of the operators, for at certain points in the narrow passage-ways alongside the tracks there were roof joists set at such an angle that one either had to drop on hands and knees to pass to another section of the line, or attempt a bit of fancy trapeze work.

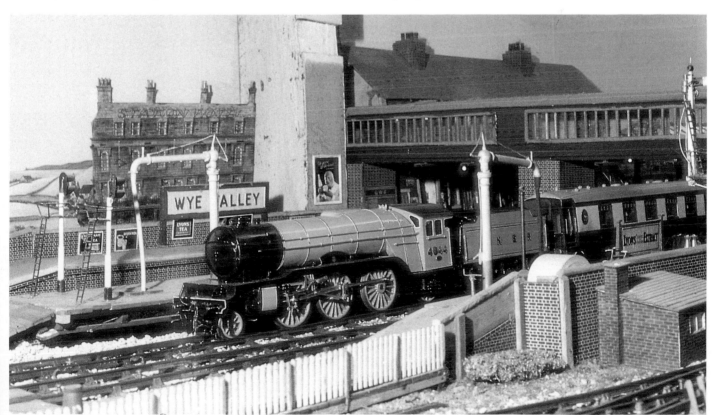

Now I am sure Fred will not mind if I describe him as being generously built, not to say portly, and I remember thinking that if he could negotiate these obstacles, they should not baffle me. At yet another point it became necessary to crawl under the base-board of the principal station, Bourne Bank, in order to reach other parts of the railway, and I marvelled at the acrobatic ease with which my host dived and twisted to reach distant parts of the railway.

Despite the handicap of impaired vision, Fred has built some of his locomotives himself; indeed, I photographed a Stanier 2-6-4T on which he was currently working. Others had been built by Phil Johnson, a man whose name I was to encounter in a variety of places and circumstances, for he is one of those men who spend a disproportionate amount of their time helping other modellers – sometimes less gifted than himself. Later I was to meet Phil and photograph his own garden railway in 'O' gauge.

Fred's railway was predominantly LMS/GWR in character, and considerable skill and observation had gone into evoking the atmosphere of such a joint line, depending not so much on minute detail as on overall impressions.

I have described Fred Marshall as being shy, and indeed his speech was at times slightly hesitant, as if he were diffident about expressing his opinions, but I was to see another side to his character when, later that evening, we settled down by the fire to chat. I have mentioned that at the time of my first stay with Ann and Fred, he ran a shop which specialised in philately, and it was not difficult to steer the conversation round to that subject; in fact it was on that occasion that I first learned the difference between stamp-collecting and philately. It became clear to me that this man knew his subject intimately, and had had extremely import-ant papers published in a world-famous philatelic journal. Warming to his subject, all the hesitancy left his voice and I listened to a man who knew and loved his subject. Knowing nothing whatsoever of philately, nevertheless I was held enthralled as Fred told the story of his pursuit of a rare example of postage stamps. It all sounded like some exciting detective story.

In due course I had to take my leave from this warm-hearted couple, and a week later had put the programme together. The photographs were passable, but I had to admit that the recorded

commentary left much to be desired, mainly due to Fred's unease before the microphone. However, if there is one thing I have learned from making these audio-visual programmes, it is not to tamper with a man's natural way of speaking. To do so is to presume to try to amend his whole personality; if he is naturally loquacious and long-winded, then, within reasonable limits, leave him to do it his way. If he is inclined to be taciturn and mono-syllabic, then let it be so. But I was concerned that the commentary did not do justice to Fred's railway and all the work he put into making it.

The answer came from Fred himself, for, having seen his own copy of the finished programme, he was strongly self-critical, and he wrote to ask me if it might be possible at some time in the future to re-record the commentary, for which purpose he would prepare a script from which he could read; he would be far more comfortable doing it that way. (Would that more people were able to perceive the beam in their own eye!). Now, if there is one thing I do try to avoid, it is working from prepared scripts, for it never sounds completely spontaneous. I prefer to conduct an extempore conversation, I acting as the link-man, and asking the silly questions. However, if a man feels happier with a prepared script – so be it – and in the event, the second attempt was highly successful, with all the hesitancy and mike-shyness gone.

For quite a while after these events I noticed that Fred's requests for the loan of these Guild presentations had ceased, yet he had been an avid supporter of the scheme, borrowing sets at frequent intervals. It was only comparatively recently that I learned that he had undergone extremely serious (and dangerous) surgery upon his eyes which – had it failed – would mean a complete loss of sight. As it is, he still had to endure permanent double-vision, but this does not seem to affect his enthusiasm. He attends shows and conventions where we often meet – driven there by his wife, and he has resumed regular borrowing of audio-visual programmes.

People like Fred Marshall and Don Wilson exercise an influence far beyond the making of a beautiful model railway; they make us who moan and grumble about our aches and pains, stop and consider how trivial are our problems compared to the Fred Marshalls of this world.

Derek Lucas

I HAVE LOST count of the number of friends I have met for the first time at the house of the late John Hart during the 25 years I knew him, but numbered among that merry band was Derek Lucas, who lived nearby, and who had a very fine clockwork layout in a spare bedroom. Being indoors, Derek had the advantage of being able to use more delicate materials for his scenery and lineside effects than is possible out in the open, and his compact railway was an impressive example of multum in parvo.

Derek and his wife are both professional musicians, so as I am a (very) amateur musician, this formed another bond. Based firmly on SOUTHERN RAILWAY practice, the continuous oval double-track layout was in coarse scale, and of course (in those days), was freed from the tyranny of wiring and control systems. There were some extremely fine examples of the model-maker's art in both locomotives and rolling stock, so that one tended to expect a superbly equipped workshop, together with lathes, sophisticated machine tools and a vast array of other implements of the dedicated model-maker. In fact, most of Derek's work was done either on the floor or the table in the lounge! (The grand piano, I was given to understand by Derek's wife, Mavis, was strictly out of bounds as a flat working surface!) But it is the hallmark of a good craftsman that he works without mess, and it was quite amazing to see the models of high quality turned out in these conditions.

One of the most arresting of these models was a tavern car, complete down to the tiniest detail of interior fittings. These tavern cars proved to be very unpopular with the travelling public, and were soon abandoned. I would imagine that one of the main objections to them was the complete absence of any windows. Doubtless, BR imagined the travelling businessman would be lulled into an illusion of being in his local pub, would lose all sense of time and space as he hurtled through the countryside, consuming vast quantities of sociable gin-and-its with his colleagues, to the huge profit of BR. What the perpetrators of these claustrophobic mobile troglodite dens failed to appreciate was that one of the compensations for the ruinous cost of meals/refreshments on a train was to be able to view the passing scenery as one imbibed refreshments at prices which would have made the owner of a Soho night-club blush for shame.

One project well-remembered was jointly undertaken by Derek Lucas and John Hart. Both wanted a Bulleid West Country Pacific, so the two men came to an agreement whereby John would built two chassis – one clockwork and one electric, while Derek would build the two bodies. This took quite some time but at length all was ready for the launching ceremony, for which S.W. Stevens-Stratten, then editor of the MODEL RAILWAY CONSTRUCTOR, was invited to perform the function of 'celebrity'. For this Steve somehow acquired two 7mm scale champagne bottles which he proposed to break over the two engines, but if memory serves me right, the builders of the beautifully finished engines drew the line at actually trying to smash the bottles on the loco bodies. However, the event turned out to be hilarious, and the two engines duly made their maiden runs at John's house. Derek named his engine WILTON, that being his wife's maiden name, while John christened his SALISBURY.

Round about this time, Derek and I found ourselves invited to give a joint talk to the BBC TV Model Railway Club at the Shepherd's Bush Centre. I cannot remember much about that, except that I felt vaguely disgruntled at the absence of Richard Baker or at least Michael Fish.

Some years later I asked Derek if I might make a Guild programme on his PINEHAVEN & ROSSHAMPTON clockwork line (which, by the way, by this time had acquired a few electric locos), and at the appointed time I turned up with all my gear – cameras (plural, be it noted) floodlights, cables, recording gear, etc, and we set to work, taking pictures under Derek's guidance, while he kept a detailed record of the contents of each shot on the clip-board for when we had to make the recorded commentary. All went well until just before Mavis called us to lunch, when it began to dawn on me that all was not well.

"Just a minute, Derek" I said "How many shots have we taken so far?"

Derek glanced at his clip-board.

"We have taken 47 pictures" he announced.

"Yes" I replied "and the maximum number of exposures on a film is 36."

Red-faced and incredulous, the J. Arthur Rank of Gauge 'O' had committed the classic boob – there was no film in the camera! The summons to lunch was not to be gainsaid, and Derek was very kind about it – we would start again after lunch, this time with a film in the camera. Curiously enough, once we re-started operations, thanks to the fact that we had detailed notes of the position of each shot, it took us about 30 minutes to accomplish what we had attempted in two hours that morning. But never before or since have I tried that trick.

There was yet another link between my own railway and Derek's in that he was one of the principal pioneers in the use of what came to be known as the 'teleguv'. The story of the teleguv has been told in great detail elsewhere, but, briefly, in 1956 – the year the Guild was formed – an ingenious clockwork enthusiast had taken the neat little governor from the old telephone dials and introduced it into the gear-train of a clockwork mechanism, with dramatic results, making possible very fine gradations of speed.

The prototype was handed to me early in 1957 by the inventor, with carte blanche to develop, and if possible market it; he did not want to be further involved. I fitted the modified mechanism into my Bassett-Lowke 4-4-0 Class 2P engine, and this is now in the possession of David East. For some time I sought the interest of firms such as Bassett-Lowke, Mills Bros., et al, but already these firms were abandoning clockwork drive, or even leaving the Gauge 'O' market altogether. It was too late.

Then something else happened which at last made this clever device accessible to all clockwork enthusiasts. A young engineer named Bob Lovell came to Crewchester on a visit, and seeing the performance of my 2P, decided that, with a little modification, the teleguv could be almost mass-produced, and within a year he had designed a version of the teleguv which could be fitted to a clockwork mechanism by any reasonably competent model engineer. I was able to track down a source of supply of these governors, and supplied them to many hundreds of clockwork operators.

Derek Lucas was quick to follow suit, but Norman Eagles, the uncrowned king of spring drive, was a reluctant convert. In time, he became a keen advocate of the system and fitted the teleguv to many of his engines on the Sherwood Section of the LMS.

Perhaps the most memorable event in the history of the teleguv was a meeting of the Guild at Keen House, the HQ of the Model Railway Club of Great Britain, where Derek and I brought along some of our teleguv locos; mine being a black five whose mechanism had been designed by Bob Lovell, and Derek brought one or two Southern engines. Before a frankly sceptical audience, these engines were put to work on the test track with a rake of coaches fitted with PTFE bearings. Having been fully wound and then sent on their way, Bob, who was supervising the affair from inside the oval, allowed the trains to come to a stand, and then lifted the engines from the track. The driving wheels turned through no more than one or two full revolutions, thus proving that the full force of the spring had been utilised. Thus was the greatest drawback to spring drive conquered, but too late to become a commercial success.

There was yet another link between myself and Derek. When the big firms like Bassett-Lowke, Hornby, etc, abandoned Gauge 'O' clockwork maintenance, there was no source of supply of springs, and over a period of some 20 years I undertook the distribution of springs throughout the hobby, supplying all types of springs to people literally all over the world. It was a mammoth undertaking, for it involved travelling to Sheffield, finding a manufacturer, and then seeing the project through, collecting the bulk order, paying for it, and then despatching and invoicing the springs to spring-starved modellers. At one stage, such was the pressure of my own work that Derek stepped in and took over one whole batch – a daunting task!

I remember a phone call during that period when Derek told me that he had approached STC (Standard Telephones and Cables) of Southgate where, after many fruitless calls he had at last been put through to management. A lugubrious voice at the other end of the line had informed Derek unhappily "No – sorry – we can't help you. Nothing here is standard; we have no telephones, and we are out of cables. Good day."

Bill Tate

THE STAIRCASE was packed with people moving up and down as I tried to make my way from the AGM of the Guild down to the exhibition floor, and there was plenty of good-humoured jostling as we went. At one particularly congested landing I became aware of a hand tugging at my sleeve and a voice with a distinctively Lancastrian accent asking "You are Jack Ray, aren't you?"

The event was a Gauge 'O' convention in the buildings of Manchester University in 1983 where even then it was being found that these commodious premises were not really adequate for the needs of convention. I turned to find a man smiling at me, and having confessed to my identity, he continued "I believe you are looking for model railways to photograph for the Guild Slide Collection? I have a Gauge 'O' Railway – it is nothing very much – but I wondered if perhaps you might like to have a look at it – –" His voice tailed off diffidently as we were swept down another flight of stairs, exchanging greetings on the way with other people moving upwards, but somehow we managed to keep together, this new acquaintance and I, until we found ourselves jammed in yet another staging post on the downward progress. Some almost instinctive impulse, possibly engendered by the fact that I was in Manchester at the time, prompted me to ask "You are not Bill Tate, are you?" His face – as the novelists say – lit up. He grinned an infectious grin at me and said "Aye – my name is Tate. I don't think we have ever met."

"No" I agreed "but of course I have heard of you, and of your railway; Millport and Selfield, isn't it?"

The Manchester Model Railway Society's annual exhibition is of course almost legendary – one of the finest shows of its kind in the country, and Bill Tate's name was almost synonymous with the MMRS. In no time at all we had arranged a tentative date for me to visit his home in order to make a Guild audio-visual programme on Millport & Selfield, but as he lived a long way distant from my own home I had to wait until I could find other business in the locality so as to make the journey economically acceptable, and this was done through the good offices of the indefatigable Joe Brown, who lived in that area, and who provided me with lodging for the night.

Bill Tate proved to be quite a personality, his infectious enthusiasm and humour making light of our labours as we moved from one vantage point to the next in order to get our pictures. Judged by today's standards, Bill's railway was, like my own Crewchester, almost archaic. It was coarse scale, and the engines, all of them good representations of their prototypes, lacked brake gear and full cab detail, but this did nothing to detract from the overall effect of a working railway system, operated every week by a faithful band of enthusiasts, using full-size block-instruments and timetables. Even while we were working, Bill insisted "We

was full of personal associations and memories, as is inevitable with such a long-lived project, and Bill spoke with great affection of some of the people who had been closely associated with the line during its long history. It has been commented before that a model railway usually represents something remembered from the builder's younger days – something no longer in existence, or changed out of recognition, and this railway of Bill's was no exception. It incorporated a branch line to Seahouses, a seaside resort on the north-east coast, where Bill and his wife, Una, had spent their honeymoon and many subsequent holidays. The little tank engine which hauled the 4-wheel coaches along that branch was a replica of the one in which he had done many footplate trips. On that picturesque branch to Seahouses the line passed through a place called Fleetham where originally a station had been planned, but in fact never built. Bill had built it! Hard by that station was a viaduct spanning a river, the area being known as Long Nanny Brow. Behind the tiny terminus at Seahouses Bill had fixed to the wall an old NER poster showing Seahouses harbour, and this made a most convincing backdrop to the scene. Although I have never been there, I could easily visualise what it had been like in those pre-war days.

Bill is no longer with us, but is affectionately remembered, especially in Manchester. He lent me an exercise book which was a full record of the evolution of the railway from its first days, packed with photographs and diagrams interspersed with a text hand-written by Bill. The last I heard was that Una still keeps the railway up on that second floor of the big house, and that weekly sessions are still run there by some of the regular operators who knew Bill well. Long may this continue as a working memorial to one of the hobby's great characters!

Post scriptum. Hardly had I written that last paragraph than the telephone rang giving me the news that Una had at last joined her husband. Thus ends yet another era in the history of well-known Gauge 'O' railways, and once again I am grateful that there was time to place it on record for others to enjoy. And enjoy it they will – for Bill's cheerful voice on the commentary ensures this!

don't take any of this too seriously – it is all very light-hearted,'' yet with almost the same breath he added ''Apart from my home and my work, the railway has been my whole life.'' He was 78 when we made that programme yet he still had the enthusiasm of a youngster, although in fact he was a sick man. Shortly after my visit to him, he was taken to hospital for what he described to me as ''a boiler wash-out and extensive re-tubing''. Although he did apparently recover from this spell in hospital, he was soon back and this time he did not return.

The railway, which he had started to build back in the 1940s

FOCUS ON OPERATION

John Castle

THE VOICE on the phone was quite unfamiliar to me. It was diffident and at same time deliberate, as from a man who thought carefully before he spoke, and it carried a slightly rural burr which gave great individuality.

Having ascertained that he was speaking to Jack Ray, the voice identified itself as belonging to John Castle, and the reason for the call soon became clear.

"I hear that you are looking for model railways to be photographed for the Guild Slide Collection, and I wondered if you might think it worth while coming to see mine?"

This was the sort of call which was all too rare, and I quickly made an appointment to visit John, who lived a good two hours' drive from my home, and when I arrived at the remote address he had given me I was immediately struck by the spick-and-span condition of his farm — everything was tidy and the paintwork on the outbuildings was sparkling and fresh. Nowhere did I see the usual heaps of rusting farm machinery which is often a feature of farms. The place looked cared-for and spoke of considerable effort by someone to keep it so.

I found John in one of the outbuildings, and immediately I identified him as the archetype of the English farmer — big, with hands like hams and a face full of all weathers. Within minutes of arrival I was made to feel at home, and John started to show me round his railway. It was a very fresh April morning and, rather apt to feel the cold, I wondered if I might need an extra woolly from the car. I need not have worried, for the room was carpeted, and an efficient heater had been switched on for some time before my arrival. As I went round with John I was amazed that the exquisitely delicate models, especially the scenery and buildings, had been fashioned by those huge hands. There was a beautiful replica of the house in which he lived, correct down to the last detail, including the garden — although John spoke ruefully of some of the miniature garden produce which was very much out of season. The station building of Canham Junction on the main line was a model of the erstwhile French Drove station near Wisbech, which John had visited, measured, and photographed so that even the number of courses of bricks was correct. The layout at that time represented a main line junction (Canham Junction)

with a branch line to a country terminus, all of which was contained in this outbuilding. At lunch-time we walked to the house where John's wife had prepared a magnificent lunch for us (farmers usually eat well, and he certainly needed good food to sustain that mighty frame of his!). He told me that the bright paintwork which adorned all the farm buildings was the work of his wife.

I found John to be a jovial character, despite all the cares and tribulations which are concomitants of a small arable farm ("I'm no barley baron, Jack!" he rumbled at me) and the day passed all too quickly.

For some years after that 1984 visit the resultant slide programme did the rounds among Guild members, until I learned that John had teamed up with a friend of German nationality, named Gerhardt ("but we call him Garry") who was a genius at electrical and electronic engineering, and the railway now extended into another room in those outbuildings. John himself was a master of improvisation, always able to perceive ways of achieving his purpose without spending a fortune, and when the two men joined forces, the results were, to say the least, spectacular. So it was that in 1992 I made a second journey to that farm, was introduced to Garry, whose English did nothing to betray his nationality, and I set to work to make a second half to the programme. A new main line terminus had been built with some fine scenery, and a goods yard and loco shed. The best was kept until the end, when the two men produced their piece de resistance – a fully working breakdown train, radio-controlled. John told me that this little masterpiece was the work of Garry, and I was given a demonstration of the whole train in action. (Later, John gave me a video of the entire procedure, from the

moment an engine became derailed at Tilbrook – all the necessary planning of the route the breakdown train had to take, emergency measures to make it possible for the train to reach the derailed engine, etc etc) but for the Guild programme we had to be content with a sequence of pictures which showed a ship being unloaded into waiting goods wagons by the quayside at Castle Garry (the new terminus). The whole operation was controlled by Garry, standing well back from the railway with his control box in his hands. Outriggers were first run out to stabilise the crane, and then the jib was slowly raised from the match-truck – the piston at the side giving a perfect imitation of the real thing, and then the huge crane swung round until the jib was over the ship's hold. The little yellow arrow on the side of the jib showed the angle of the jib throughout the entire process. The multi-cable hook gradually dropped until it could be attached to the crate, and then the whole routine was repeated in reverse, until the crate was lowered gently and accurately into the wagon which, incidentally, was only just large enough to take it. At no time, (except to feed the hook under the ring on the crate) did John or Garry lay a finger on any part of the machinery, and I watched, fascinated as the crane, now relieved of its load, folded itself up until the jib was lying once again on the match-truck, and the outriggers were pushed back into their housing underneath.

I have made many of these programmes, but I know of none where the commentary does more to warm the audience to the speaker, for John's great good humour and enthusiasm come across in a remarkable way. Many a letter has come back with this programme, telling me of the delighted chuckles from the audience as they listened to John, and watched the pictures of his colourful railway.

Ronnie Hoare

I T IS EASIER, we are told on very high authority, for a camel to pass through the eye of a needle than for a rich man to enter into the Kingdom of Heaven. Setting aside for the moment the purely academic question as to the camel's desire to thread itself, there is an underlying truth in the contention, for wealth brings with it problems quite as serious (if different) as poverty.

Colonel Ronnie Hoare was undoubtedly a wealthy man, and although many speculative rumours prevailed as to the extent of his wealth, they are irrelevant here, for I am more concerned with the man himself, the man who, inspired by the late Stanley Norris, set out to start where Norris finished. Articles and pictures began to appear in model railway magazines showing a superbly detailed model railway, but with no mention of the owner. There were a few privileged people, usually within the Gauge 'O' Guild – of which the Colonel was a member – who had been able to visit the railway, and stories abounded, telling of the fabulous cost of the railway, and the almost unbelievable security which surrounded it.

Let me make it quite clear that although I corresponded with Ronnie Hoare over a period of some years, and spent three days as his guest shortly before he died, I never addressed him by his first name; only his close friends and family did this. Yet, now he is no longer with us, it is with no disrespect – rather with affection – that I speak of him, as did most people, as Ronnie Hoare.

At the time when the Bromford and High Peak Railway first began to reach the model press, the figure of Ronnie Hoare was a shadowy one, and there were few who could speak of him from first-hand contact. Shortly after I started the Guild slide/cassette scheme I was asked if I had plans to make a programme on Colonel Hoare's railway. The answer was no, but then neither had I any plans to visit the vaults of the Bank of England. I had no idea of how one went about breaching this impregnable fortress, but a little judicious enquiry led me to Hugh Joslin, who appeared to be the Colonel's right-hand man, and in due course I received a most pleasant letter from Hugh, telling me that he had asked the Colonel for his views concerning a Guild programme, and had received his assent. Hugh went on to point out that the insurance policy on the railway dictated the very tightest security, including such provisos that no-one under 16 (I think) was to be allowed in the building; that the owner's name was not to be mentioned, either verbally in any interview, or in articles on the railway. Only certain named persons were permitted to handle the vast console which controlled the system, and so on. Unfortunately, the dates when I could get to the locality coincided with one of the Colonel's frequent trips abroad, and Hugh conveyed to me the Colonel's regret that he would be unable to entertain me personally. I have a shrewd idea that this was a ploy by which Hoare

was able to get an 'advance report' from his staff on first-time visitors who were unknown to him! Be that as it may, I booked an hotel nearby, where the proprietor proved to be an ex-driver on the Somerset and Dorset Railway, and this nearly threatened my punctuality at the Colonel's railway, for I was fascinated by my host's stories of driving over the Mendips in steam days.

When at last I arrived at the building which (then) housed the railway, I had to admit that it was impressive. There were three people present on that occasion, apart from myself; Hugh Joslin, John Macklie, and a cheery personality named George, who was responsible for most of the buildings and lineside effects. John Macklie was the electronics wizard of the line. Hugh, it appeared, had served in Hoare's old Regiment and was a greatly valued friend and henchman.

I suppose one of the first things to strike the visitor was the elaborate lighting, which was achieved by a series of battens running across the large room at intervals, each one carrying a series of carefully focused spotlights. The sheer cost of this complicated lighting was daunting, and curiously enough it led to numerous problems when I started taking photographs. Hugh soon produced a variety of flood-lights to augment the overall light, so I was able to dispense with my own.

The whole thing was magnificent, from the extraordinary wealth of detail to the trains themselves, which represented all four main groups. Models by Vic Green, Stanley Beeson, and other famous names abounded, and the massive console was like something from the control room of an atomic power station. Apart from the 7mm railway, there were other miniature locomotives in that large room, varying from 2½" gauge to much larger passenger carrying engines.

And here I have to admit to a slight disappointment. I spent two quite delightful days making that Guild programme, and everything I saw delighted me. It was a rich man's toy. There was one feature on that vast layout which I just could not accept – the spiral of 6' radius curves which led from the low level of Bromford to the higher level of High Peak! To my mind, the sight of a magnificent Gresley Pacific hauling a set of 10 Pullmans round the incredibly tight circle was an anticlimax, yet it was a prominent feature on the railway. Apart from this, the whole effect was quite overwhelming, and I found in Hugh Joslin a most amenable companion. He took me home to meet his wife, who gave me lunch, and altogether it was an unforgettable two days, with much work – and much laughter – until the time came for my return home to await the slides from the processors.

In due course these came back and I was able to put these together, with a copy sent to the Colonel. It was this which led to a sporadic correspondence over the next eight years, during which

Hoare spoke frequently of a possible return visit, when he could entertain me personally, but as the railway was being moved to a new site, this would have to be deferred until it was once more assembled and running again. During this time I would phone Hugh Joslin from time to time, and eventually the time came when we might plan that second visit.

However, two events further postponed the trip, the first being Hugh's sudden and tragic death. I had been talking to him on the phone one evening when he enthusiastically told me that 'we will be ready for you very soon now' – and two days later, Hugh had gone. The second event was the Colonel's serious heart attack which landed him in hospital shortly before Christmas 1988. Our meeting had been arranged for January 1989, and just after Christmas '88 I had a letter assuring me that his illness did not mean delaying my visit, and that he wanted to spend as much time as possible with me. I shall never know exactly what that effort cost him, for he was a mortally sick man, yet he insisted on coming to the hotel where he had booked me quite lavish accommodation. On the Friday of my arrival he was driven to the hotel by a chauffeur, and accompanied by a nurse, who wheeled him into the lounge where I was awaiting his arrival. He was 75 then, and his voice was quiet, as would be expected from one who had just survived a major heart attack, but his warmth was quite disarming. Very soon we moved to the restaurant, (where the nurse was given another table), and we were chatting enthusiastically about all manner of things – not all necessarily railway topics. He was a good listener as well as entertaining talker, and gave the impression that he found what I had to say of great interest, which is a rare gift. He ate little, but seemed to take more pleasure from his glass than from his plate, until it was time for him to return home to his flat. I was to call for him the following morning when

we would go to the new site of the railway, and I wondered just which of his many cars we would travel in. Not a bit of it! He insisted on riding in my old banger, and I had almost to carry him from the steps of his flat to the car. On the way he pointed out various places where cameras were hidden, keeping constant watch on speeding motorists, and when I asked him how it was he was so well-informed, he chuckled, saying "I was on the County Council when we planned them!"

We spent the day on the railway, taking fresh photographs, and he was almost like a schoolboy, showing me the new models he had acquired, and telling me of those he had commissioned and were not yet ready. In the evening he had another engagement and handed me over to John Macklie who was detailed to take me to a favourite restaurant and give me dinner.

Sunday morning saw me at the flat where 'elevenses' consisted of the almost statutory champagne, and more chat. Although it was January, the French windows were open on to the balcony which commanded a fine seascape. All round the walls were paintings of high-powered racing cars and boats, and I already knew of Hoare's interest in these matters. What I did not know is that Graham Hill was one of his drivers. Other facets of this quiet man's life were revealed that morning, such as his youthful compulsive desire to join the Army, rather than follow in his father's footsteps. (His father had been Chairman of the Metropolitan Railway).

"I hope you don't mind" he announced, almost apologetically, "but I have booked lunch at your hotel – and invited Stan Beeson and his wife to meet you." Did I mind!

I then got out my recording gear and we recorded his commentary on the pictures I had taken on the previous day, arranging the microphone so that he could speak easily from his wheel chair.

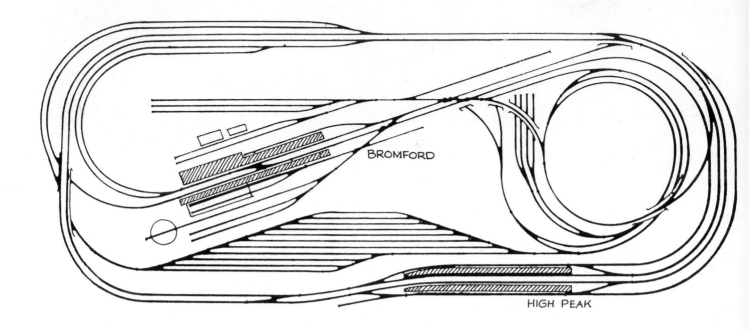

BROMFORD

HIGH PEAK

When I had packed all the equipment up and returned it to my car, Ronnie Hoare told me enthusiastically of his latest purchase. He had bought, lock, stock and barrel, a 00 layout, including 400 private owner wagons.

"You must come and see it, Jack" he insisted. "John Mackie is going to bring it out to Monte Carlo and assemble it there for me as I shall be there for some time. I'll let you know when it is ready."

Perhaps we both knew that this was unlikely, but the offer was perfectly genuine. I think he knew that he was unlikely to survive the year, and indeed he died only a few months later. And anyway, Monte Carlo is not one of my regular social haunts; somehow I feel that my frayed collar and shapeless flannels would be hardly suitable for the Principality.

However, that final lunch was memorable. No sooner had we entered the restaurant and I had been introduced to Stan and Mrs. Beeson, than the inevitable champagne appeared – compliments of the management – while a very attractive young lady entertained us discreetly on a full-sized orchestral harp! That was my only meeting with the great Stan Beeson, and I have the happiest memories of the event. Between him and Ronnie Hoare there was quite clearly a close friendship, and I think we all enjoyed that gathering enormously, although once again I noticed that Hoare ate next to nothing.

I came away from that visit with a sense of an opportunity taken which would perhaps not be repeated, and in this I was right. Both Hoare and Beeson died that year. Of the model railway I could say much, for it was an example of just what a rich man could do when money was no object. But 'starting where Norris had finished' – never! In all humility, and with the greatest respect and even affection for Colonel Ronnie Hoare, the railway lacked the vision of Norris. Although a highly skilled and knowledgable man on the internal combustion engine, I saw no evidence of personal involvement in the building of engines and rolling stock to the extent I saw on the Norris railway, and that height-gaining spiral rather stuck in my throat. That he loved his railway there was not a shadow of doubt, and shortly before he died he sent me a folio of full-plate photographs of most of his engines, together with their history. These were superb photographs taken with the Linhoff large-format camera, of which he showed me two while I was with him. He always preferred black and white to colour for his locomotive pictures.

Whatever one may say of this magnificent model railway, the man himself was in every way a great gentleman in every sense of that overworked word; courteous, thoughtful for the comfort of others, generous to a degree, and unstinting in his hospitality. There will be those who decry the wealthy dilettante – the man who pays others to build his models (as indeed I do in a more modest way) but in so doing he enabled the great model builders whom he patronised to practise their craft, and without such men, these giants, such as Stanley Beeson or Vic Green could not work. And the hobby would be the poorer for it.

125

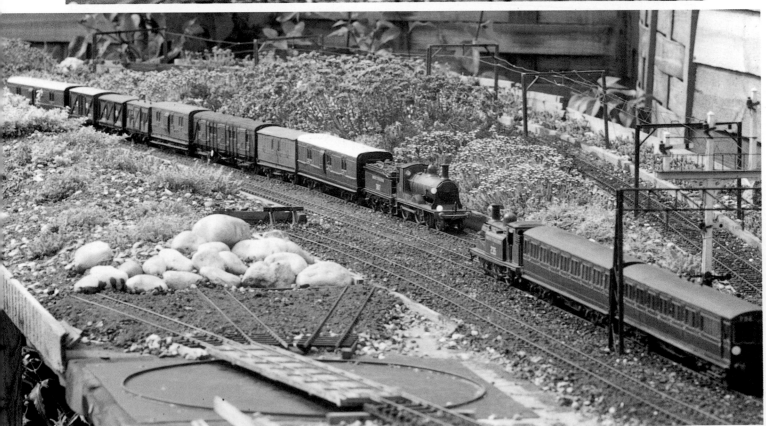

Eddie Bye

EDDIE BYE has a most disturbing habit of saying nothing. Where other people would, more or less tactfully, point out the shortcomings of my own railway, Eddie just stands and looks at the offending feature, and says nothing – very, VERY loudly. I can sense the vibrations more clearly than if he had said something like "That facing point is a bit naughty, isn't it?" He is not always right, but most of the time he is – uncomfortably right – and the result is that I have to tear up months of work and start again.

It was at John Hart's house that we first met, Eddie Bye then being a very young man, and I well into middle age. It was one of those spontaneous and inexplicable rapports which do happen, and although our friendship has been liberally larded with mutual insults, it has proved durable. Living south of the Thames, it is not surprising to find him a staunch SOUTHERN fan, and his own model railway is almost exclusively Southern. His profession did little to suggest engineering skills, for he is a business management consultant, but his early days under the considerable influence of John Hart set his feet firmly on the road to model-building.

Although we frequently met at John's house, I never saw his own model railway until he moved away from Surbiton, and similarly, although he did pay one visit to the old Crewchester (clockwork) railway, it was not until after 1982, when I turned to 2-rail electric power that his periodic visits started. It was at that time that I realised that, for all his outwardly cynical attitude, not surprising in view of his profession, his basic attitude to model railways was romantic and imaginative in the extreme. He 'lived' his railway, seeing in his mind all that was missing in the models – the steam and smoke – the smell of coal and oil – and all that went to the atmosphere of the steam age. The simplest things could give him intense pleasure, such as an ordinary shunting movement, or a train leaning into a curve. The lack of detail detracted not one iota from his sense of 'realism', although he is very quick to appreciate the craftsmanship of such people as Vic Green, Stan Beeson, or Bernard Miller. His own skills are far from inconsiderable, and some of his workmanship earned him high praise from John Hart. Especially was this so with his painting, lining, and lettering of both engines and coaches, in which craft he was a fervent admirer of the late Bernard Miller. Eddie said to me once

"On the one occasion when I met Bernard, I asked him how he managed to do such exquisite lining, and Bernard told me that he could certainly not do it when sober. At least half a bottle of claret had to be consumed before Bernard would attempt any tricky lining-out job!"

I remember also Eddie's own reply when I asked him how he had done a remarkable job of lining-out a set of Southern coaches. He said "I spend ten minutes at least stirring the paint until it has reached the ideal consistency, then I take a deep drag on my cigarette, hold my breath, fill the ruling pen, and draw the line, only breathing again when I reach the end." I know the feeling!

Moves of house have interrupted the development of Eddie's railway, but basically, the principal theme remains constant, with Stonemouth as the main terminal station, and one line going ultimately to a connection with my own railway, with Rockhill (Exchange) forming the link. In fact, he built a beautiful set of SR mainline coaches, bearing destination boards marked STONE-HAVEN – PORT TRENTON. THE PORTS EXPRESS. This train he brings with him when visiting Crewchester and we have included on one of the Crewchester videos the complete journey, starting from Stonemouth, running over NORTH AND SOUTH JUNCTION metals and then continuing from Rockhill to Port Trenton on my own line. Some journey, when it is remembered that 125 miles separate our two homes!

It is very tempting to write of all the work Eddie has done for my own railway, but this chapter is about his railway, and I am quite sure that he would have made greater progress on this had he spent less time doing things for me. He learned much of his modelling skills from John Hart and has developed from that invaluable apprenticeship his own particular techniques, which, with his inventive mind, have led to some quite remarkable results. One recent example comes to mind.

With electric propulsion, it is no great problem to take current to the interior of the coaches and illumine them during night-time sessions. It can be extremely rewarding to run a nocturnal session, watching the train travelling through the night, and coming into a lamplit station. The trouble is that, as the controller is turned down to bring the train to a stand at the platform, the lights also dim and eventually go out. The effect is lost. But the fact that Eddie's layout is Southern, places a trump card in his hand, which he has played with great effect. His engines are powered on the 2-rail system, but, being Southern, he is perfectly justified in adding a third, outside 'power' rail, and it from this that he draws from a secondary circuit the power for his coach interior lighting. This, of course, is not affected by the traction circuit, so the lighted coaches still sparkle even when the train comes to rest at stations – or elsewhere.

But he has taken the principle even further, fitting little LEDs as tail-lamps and headlamps to the front and rear of his trains, thereby adding yet another dimension to his railway. All his signals (semaphores) are also lighted, so at night time the railway is a veritable fairyland of twinkling lights.

He has never been noticeably in favour of fine-scale, and for most of the time he has stuck to dependable 28mm b-b wheel standards. However, his son, Andrew shows great interest in the railway, and will one day probably inherit it. Knowing that by the time that happens, coarse scale is likely to be obsolescent, Eddie has converted all his engines and rolling stock to fine standards – an example of forethought and unselfishness which is somewhat rare in my experience.

Progress is necessarily slow on the latest layout, for Eddie's profession makes very heavy demands on his time and energy, but it will be well worth waiting for. I look back with some nostalgia to his last layout, which included a highly unusual feature – the Willow End branch which, after leaving Stonemouth Town, left the main line and climbed up to the little terminus of Willow End. The unusual part of this single-track branch was that it was worked by an electric set, taking its current from an overhead catenary – based on the old line which used to run to Crystal Palace (High Level) station. I never thought I would enthuse about an electric train, but there were times when that little three-car set was pure magic. Imagine sitting at Stonemouth in the gathering dusk, towards the end of an operating session, with the last of the steam trains in, and stabled. The very last working of the branch train brought it into the main through-platform at Stone-

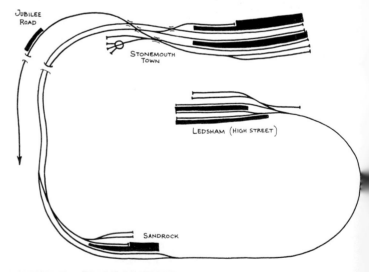

mouth, after which it would make one last trip to Stonemouth Harbour before returning to the Town station. Normally, that train would run into the bay, but this run was different. Turning up the controller, one could see in the distance the arcing of the pantograph in the damp early evening air, with flashes of blue light coming from the wheels as the train ran over the maze of double-slips at the station throat, the motor purring and the wheels clattering over the joints, until it ran into the long platform. It would take a very biased mind not to be moved by the sheer convincing realism of that scene.

Ken Brennan

GOG Slide collection No. 99

KEN BRENNAN – the name under the signature on the letter seemed vaguely familiar – but I just could not associate it with anyone I had met or even corresponded with. He was clearly a member of the Gauge 'O' Guild, and from his letter it appeared that he had to present an evening of entertainment to a somewhat specialised audience in the Shropshire town where he was then living – and could I suggest a Guild slide/cassette programme which might fill the bill? When I had had time to ponder Ken's specific requirements a little longer I realised that none of the existing Guild programmes was really suitable, but it might be possible to put together a sequence of slides which would be tailor-made, and to which I could record a commentary.

This special programme was duly compiled and despatched to Ken, and was shown to his audience who, it appeared, enjoyed it – or at least parts of it.

Ken Brennan – Ken Brennan – why did that name sound so familiar to me? For some time I puzzled over this question until one day when Ken and I were speaking on the phone, he mentioned his friendship with Frank Roomes, and suddenly everything fell into place. I had been to Frank's home on two occasions, one in Hertfordshire, and the more recent one in Norfolk, and included in Frank's Gauge 'O' model railway was a station named Kenbrennan Castle. Frank had acquired this station from Ken and had named it thus for obvious reasons.

It was at this time that Ralph was Chairman of the Barnet Model Railway Society, and contingents from this club would often visit Ralph's house to run his railway. These sessions, I regret to say, were not always the circumspect affairs which purists demand when running a railway. Certainly a good time was had by all, which is justification for any session, but the day tended to move towards a sort of free-for-all whereby the operator at each section did his level best to throw the others into confusion by despatching as many trains into the next section as he possibly could. Ralph freely admitted that the system needed a proper timetable and inter-section communications, for at the time it was all rather free-lance, with trains being passed between sections by means of verbal signals.

Thus one would hear Peterborough calling King's Cross "Can you accept a parcels train?", followed by harrassed response from King's Cross "No – I'm completely bunged up here – you'll have to wait." Meanwhile Grantham would be complaining bitterly to Doncaster that he couldn't accept anything more until Doncaster took that pickup goods he offered half an hour ago!

Such were the demands of Ralph's work that he had little spare time for the requisite planning of an orderly timetable; indeed, it took him all his time just to keep this vast system in working order.

The railway necessarily ran over several levels, some of which were difficult of access, and except for the stations, there was no scenery. Each station and its approaches, however, was a very faithful representation of its prototype, an example being Peterborough North (the old train-shed of course). The southern

approaches included the familiar landmark of the River Nen bridge, while to the north of the station lay the long series of bric arches carrying the road over the tracks. The signalling was purel cosmetic, but lent an air of realism to the scene. Such a syster could easily have become unmanageable by anything less than highly experienced team of operators, but Ralph had great simplified matters by having all but the most inaccessible point controlled by lineside switches, coloured blue for down and re for up movements. Sidings, etc were coloured yellow, while cros overs between up and down were dual-coloured red and blue.

A bewildering array of locomotives and rolling stock was avai able for the train service, and I cannot remember ever seeing model railway with the sheer quantity of engines, coaches, an goods vehicles. It was quite a common sight, for instance, to se three arrivals lying in King's Cross, each with an express loco the buffer stops, while two trains stood ready for departure, or perhaps with an A4 at the head, and another with a large-boil Atlantic. On the loco sidings there would be a Klondyke, a bra of A3s, a D2, and a Peppercorn A1. This pattern was more or le repeated at other stations where there was a MPD, and Doncast would boast six or seven more assorted engines. Just about eve type of train was represented, with several Pullman sets, rakes Gresley teak main line stock; ECJR stock was also seen, while t occasional LMS train would be found running out of Sheffiel M&GN was also represented; in fact it was almost impossible think of any type of train which once ran over those metals whi could not be seen here in miniature.

133

My most vivid memory of visiting this railway was the first occasion when we went there en masse – two packed car-loads of Crewchester MRC members.

Ralph Cooper's wife was quite the most lavish hostess we ever encountered on our club visits, for not only was she accustomed to entertaining, but knew all about the tastes and appetites of young growing lads. So, after arriving and being fortified by a variety of cakes and drinks, we all clambered up into the loft, where Ralph organised us, appointing members to various section controls, and explaining how they worked. It rather resembled schoolboys being let loose in the tuck-shop, for here they were faced with such a choice of trains as had never before come their way.

Once the boys had familiarised themselves with the controls of their sections, trains began to move, and it was then that Ralph stood back in surprise as he saw his railway being run in a way he had never seen before. It was not that Crewchester members were paragons of circumspection, or that they displayed any special genius for operating the trains themselves: it was the verbal exchanges between the sections which astonished Ralph. It has to be remembered that the Crewchester Railway had a full series of block bells and instruments, so the boys were completely familiar with the block codes. In the absence of block bells and peggers, we all quickly adapted to a sort of verbal shorthand, dispensing with the single-bell 'call attention', but prefixing every message with the name of the station being called. Thus, when Peterborough had an express passenger train for King's Cross, instead of the rather untidy "King's Cross – can you take an express passenger?" to which the reply would be "Half a mo' – give me time to clear platform 3." – etc etc, what was heard was Peterborough speaking to King's Cross – "King's Cross – FOUR!"

To which King's Cross would acknowledge by saying "FOUR, Peterborough." Two or three minutes later, Peterborough would start his train on its way to King's Cross, and as it passd over the Nene bridge, he would call out "King's Cross – TWO!" King's Cross would answer "TWO, Peterborough" and the train would pass from Peterborough's control to King's Cross control. When the train had arrived in the terminus, King's Cross would call out "Peterborough – TWO – ONE", to which Peterborough would acknowledge "TWO – ONE, King's Cross."

This pattern was being repeated all over the loft between the sections, and the trains moved on their appointed ways smoothly and with little or no conversation. Very occasionally a hold-up might occur somewhere, causing a slight delay, and questions would be asked. Ralph would quickly come to the rescue, being thoroughly conversant with the places where electrical or other problems were likely to arise.

To those who are familiar with the block codes, all this will be immediately clear and simple. To others, unversed in block procedure, it will sound like gobbledegook – and that is exactly how it appeared to Ralph. Later, he said "Your chaps must come here and teach the Barnet boys how to operate the railway. I never saw my railway run so efficiently before!" Not for the first time, I was rather proud of my boys.

Once we sent a non-stop express direct from Newcastle, via York, to London – a very special and rare occasion for it meant that every station en route had to have a clear path for the train, which was to be given absolute priority. The purpose of the exercise was simply to ascertain the actual running time between the two termini, bearing in mind that few model railways have a run exceeding, say, two minutes' running time between stations. The train took EIGHT MINUTES to complete the run non-stop!

At the end of the session – with a two-hour journey still before us and anxious parents waiting at home – we would all troop downstairs to find the dining room table laden with just about every imaginable kind of buffet-type food. What it had cost Helen in terms of time alone was impossible to guess, but combined with the exhilarating experience of taking part in that running session, and the warm hospitality of Ralph and Helen, it is little wonder that before long the cry would be heard at Crewchester "When are we going to Barnet again?"

Those boys are all middle-aged now, while Ralph and I are old men. But there can be no members of the Crewchester MRC who, however long they live, will ever forget those magic days when we went to Barnet to run Ralph Cooper's magnificent 00 gauge model railway, and when these 'boys' come back to see me now, they will often ask "Do you ever hear from Ralph Cooper nowadays?"

Indeed I do!

OTHER SCALES
Leslie Tovell
N Gauge

TO MOST of us ordinary mortals, electrics and electronics are an alien science, the rudiments of which we have perforce to master in order that our trains shall move. For Leslie Tovell however the wiring needed for even a complex model railway was mere child's play, for Leslie was an organ builder. Lest that may puzzle some readers, let me illustrate what I mean by relating an amusing personal anecdote.

For me, electrical matters are a mystery which have always baffled me, and I have stood for hours amid a tangle of wires, trying to fathom out just where they led and what they did. John Hart, infinitely patient, used to try to explain these things to me, yet despite his lucid explanations a glazed look would come over my eyes and he would sigh – and change the subject. One day I took him into our large Parish Church where I was sub-organist,

and, at his request I unlocked the huge 3-manual console, and played for a while, showing off like mad and demonstrating the many tonal effects possible. When I stopped, I looked round to see if John was still conscious, or even still among those present. I saw him standing behind me with a puzzled frown on his brow. He said "Jack – you say that the control panel at Broadway on my railway defeats you, yet I have been watching you operating the most bewilderingly complex control panel I have ever seen, simultaneously playing a three-keyboard instrument, plus pedals – a mass of incomprehensible stops, tabs, switches, buttons and pedals."

Well, I am sure that this proves something or other. I have been a church organist most of my life and it comes almost as second nature to play them; I am just not conscious of any complexity of electrics. Maybe this is also true of people who have grown up in the world of electrics, and the electrical system of a large modern church organ is a nightmare of electrical wizardry

I think Brian Yallup must be a great favourite among exhibition organisers for his demands for space are minimal, and the time needed to set up or dismantle his layout are almost negligible, for it takes him all of five minutes to erect the layout itself, and perhaps another fifteen to place the vehicles on the tracks in the fiddle-yard. Compare this with an exhibition-layout in Gauge 'O', where a lorry is often necessary for transport, and it can take all night to assemble it, test it, and have it in perfect running order by the time the show opens to the public.

All Brian's engines and rolling stock are contained in a neat wooden cabinet of sliding drawers which can be carried in one hand. The railway is controlled from the fiddle-yard at the rear of the continuous circuit by Compspeed controllers modified to 9 volts DC. On the public viewing side there is a through station with its concomitant goods yard and a wealth of extremely attractive rural scenery. At each end the line runs into a tunnel, the formation of the land fully justifying the tunnels, and at one end, where the goods yard lies, there are one or two factories, warehouses, etc, whilst at the other end there is a little church perched on the hillside. Between these features is the village itself with the general store and High Street, all modelled in this diminutive scale so perfectly that when I have shown the slides to an audience, people have commented that it is impossible to see what scale it is. For myself, I was left in no doubt, for my limited photographic skills were sorely tested when I tried to get in close. It is a measure of Brian's good nature and patience that when I expressed dissatisfaction with my first attempts, he willingly agreed to put the layout at my disposal so that I could come again and take a series of experimental shots in order to determine the best lighting, lens, or combination of lenses. Extremely patient and forbearing too was Brian's wife, Joyce, who uncomplainingly allowed me to wreck her lounge by erecting screen and projector so that we could examine the latest attempts. She even joined in as an adjudicator when Brian and I gave each picture marks out of ten! I was rather grateful in the circumstances that this layout was not 200 miles away from my own home. I think I learned more about macro-photography on that ISTRANE layout than in all the years I have been photographing model railways in larger scales.

As I departed Brian's house after one of my visits he told me ''There is a man who is building a 'Z' gauge layout in fine-scale, would you believe!''

I plucked a hair from the rapidly diminishing stock on my head and handed it to Brian.

''Give this to him'' I said. ''He can use it for a flange''.

''No good'' grinned Brian – ''too big!''

Being an engineer by profession, modelling gave him few problems and the neatness of his workmanship reflects his professional skills. His 'N' Gauge activities started during the 1960s and continued up until the mid-1980s when he turned to the even smaller scale of 'Z', which is 1.4mm = 1ft. For Brian, obviously 'small is beautiful'. He had started exhibiting his GLENBY layout in 'N' Gauge during the 1970s, and when ISTRANE came into being, that in turn started on the rounds of the exhibition circuit, where it has been seen from as far north as Warley and as far south as Southampton.

When Brian first started in 'Z' Gauge there were virtually no commercially available models in British outline, so he would buy a continental model, remove the Marklin chassis, discard the body, and scratch-build his British outline model. What I found quite astonishing was the smoothness of running in these tiny models, and the gentle starts and stops to the trains.

138

Peter Denny

Narrow Gauge + 00

THE COUNTRY PARSON has been portrayed so often in romantic fiction, stage comedy, and television, that one is led to expect something of the type played by Alec Guinness in 'Kind Hearts and Coronets', an unworldly aesthete with little or no practical skills, absorbed in matters of scholarship and things spiritual. Thanks to his prolific writings, Peter Denny has not only become a popular and much-admired figure in the world of model railways, but has apparently transcended all barriers within the hobby, be they of gauge, standards, locale, or nationality. If proof of this universal affection for Peter Denny and his railways were needed, it would be found in the increasingly frequent enquiries I received from people within the Gauge 'O' Guild who borrowed the slide programmes, on the lines of "Are you going to do a programme on Peter Denny?" And the matter laid for some years on my conscience, like that promise to the wife to put up badly-needed shelves in the kitchen – something I fully intended to do – as soon as I could get round to it.

But how does one go about contacting this patriarch of model railways? Back in 1950, when I was just starting to take the model railways magazines, I remember reading an article by Peter Denny on his Buckingham branch, and was deeply impressed by the realism of the illustrations. The text was unusually 'readable' – something which cannot be said of all articles (or books) on model railway subjects. Over the years I read many articles by Peter, finding both enjoyment and inspiration in them, but I had never met him, and had no idea where he lived, or what was his profession. Latterly I discovered that he was a parson, and that he lived somewhere in the West Country, and then of course followed various reports from people who had been to see him. As usual, these opinions covered a strangely incompatible range, from "Withdrawn – inaccessible" to "extremely pleasant – hospitable" etc. This has happened so often in my experience that I am reminded of the fable of the two travellers who arrived in a strange town, sought out one of the elders, and questioned him – "What are the people like in this town?" To which the wise old man answered "How did you find the people in your last town?" The first man replied "Oh, they were a miserable, unfriendly lot." The second man disagreed. "I found them very pleasant – warm-hearted and friendly." The old man smiled at both the travellers. "I think" he said "you will find them much the same here."

It was Joff Bullen who helped me over the first hurdle, for he told me that he was a fairly regular visitor and operator at Mr Denny's house, and he would see how Peter reacted to the idea of being included in a Guild programme. Things began to fall into place when Joff phoned me to say that he had seen Mr Denny on the previous day, and that I would be made very welcome. Further – realising the long journey I had to make – Joff and his wife offered me hospitality for as long as I wanted to stay in the West Country, thereby enabling me to plan other programmes in the area, including Joff's own line.

This I quickly followed up by writing to Peter Denny, confirming dates, and equally promptly I received a very kind letter from him, agreeing. As there were two layouts involved I had asked if I might come on two days so as to cover both, and to this Peter readily agreed.

Those who know the West Country well will know that when it decides to rain there, it doesn't believe in doing things by half! That May week when I set out for the west, once I had passed through Wiltshire I ran into the really nasty stuff – sheets of blinding rain swept across the moors, driven by squalls coming in off the Atlantic. And so it continued both day and night! I have commented elsewhere how the Weather Man seems to be a Gauge 'O' chap, for no matter what the general weather pattern, at the crucial moment, like Moses crossing dry-shod over the Red Sea, the clouds roll back and the nastiness goes away while I take my photographs! (Peter himself might have reservations about this assertion, possibly reminding me that the Devil looks after his own!).

I had arranged to be with Peter on the Thursday and Friday of that busy week, while in the meantime I occupied the Tuesday in photographing Joff Bullen's railway (indoors), the rain still coming down in torrents all day. Wednesday saw me with Jack Patterson, whose indoor/outdoor railway threatened to become my first-ever rain-stopped-play effort. As we sat in Jack's lounge watching the rain cascading down the windows, I began to have serious fears that this whole trip was going to be a washout and waste of time and travelling. Oh me of little faith! As I sat listening to Jack's seafaring experiences (he was the RN signaller who first spotted the Bismark which led to the chase and destruction of that vessel) I soon forgot the weather, until around noon, I suddenly caught Jack's arm and pointed outside to where the sky displayed a patch of blue 'sufficient to patch a sailor's trousers'. Sure enough, the clouds dispersed and we were able to take the photographs in some two hours. At precisely the moment (4pm) when we had returned the last vehicle under cover, the heavens opened, and it rained without ceasing for 15 hours.

Thursday dawned bright and fair, with warm sunshine – the only day that week! Having found Peter's address I then discovered that owing to a misunderstanding I had arrived half an hour before I was expected. The Rev Peter Denny may be retired, but he is far from unemployed; he had things to do, so after excusing himself, he left me in the sunlit garden where I busied myself picking up wet leaves from the tracks under the shrubberies. This, of course was the outdoor Gauge 'O' track, called The Tralee Valley Light Railway – a narrow-gauge system which wound its picturesque way through a steeply sloping garden.

When Peter returned, I think we were both a trifle shy of each other at what was our first meeting, even though we had both read each other's books, but, such is the magic of the shared interest in a common hobby that within half an hour we were completely at ease, and revelling in the unexpected sunshine. As the forecast told of further heavy rain to come we decided to photograph the garden line while the sun shone, leaving the 4mm indoor line until the morrow.

It was, to say the least – a most unusual day for me, for all the locomotives were battery driven, controlled from the cab much as the old clockwork locomotives were – that is, with a brake lever and a reversing lever, both easy to reach, especially as the maximum speed was about 15mph. What amazed me most about the whole thing was Peter's inventive improvisation; everything on that railway, apart from the wheels, was the work of his own hands. He told me that he never enjoyed making up kits, preferring the satisfaction of making everything for himself. At almost every turn I saw examples of how Peter had adapted all manner of things to his purpose. For example, the old period disc signals were perfectly represented by Meccano wheels, mounted on high posts. Where a bridge spanned a concrete path, he had rigged up a counterweight device whereby when the bridge was lifted, a barrier came on to the track preventing any train from plunging over the edge. With battery drive there was no way of interrupting the power source, and at the modest pace these little trains moved, no harm would befall them if they struck the barrier.

In the fullness of time Mrs Denny brought us coffee, and as we sat in the warm sunlight enjoying the brief break, yet again I had to pinch myself at this almost unbelievable way of spending my retirement! How many people, I wondered, who had been reading of this man and his railways for half a century, would envy me this experience!

So the day passed until, my photography completed, we went indoors to record the commentary. As would be expected from a parson, this presented no problems, and in no time we had brought the recording to a close. I took my leave – temporarily – and set off through the Cornish countryside to my pied-a-terre with Joff and Mary Bullen until the next morning.

Sure enough, the rain returned, but all I now had to do was to

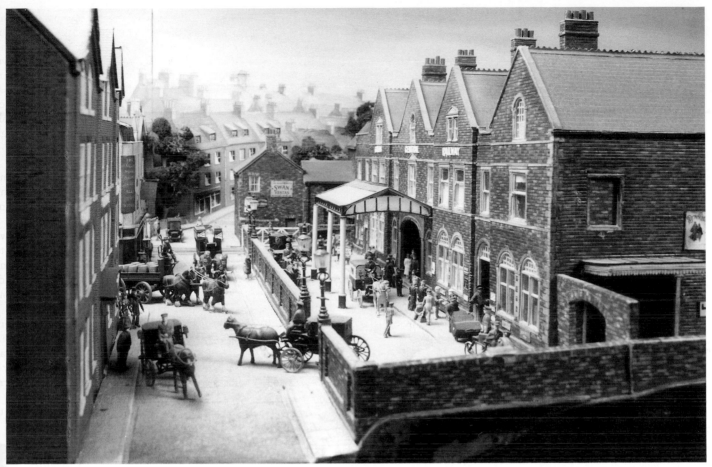

Buckingham station forecourt.
Photo – R. Prattley

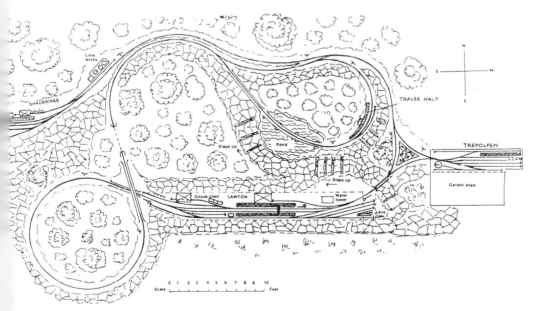

Track plan of the outdoor narrow gauge line.

photograph the indoor railway – the famous Buckingham Central branch. This was housed in a spare room, and it seemed to me that one day would be pitifully inadequate to obtain half the pictures which presented themselves. Peter had considerately mapped out a sequence of shots for me to take, which smoothed my path enormously, but as we made our way round this amazing railway I was constantly asking Peter if I could add one – two – or even three extra shots to the list. He commented "You are very thorough, aren't you!" and I replied "I have never been here before, and the chances are I may never be able to come again; I dare not miss a single detail, Peter. Nor would the people who watch the programme ever forgive me if I skimped this opportunity."

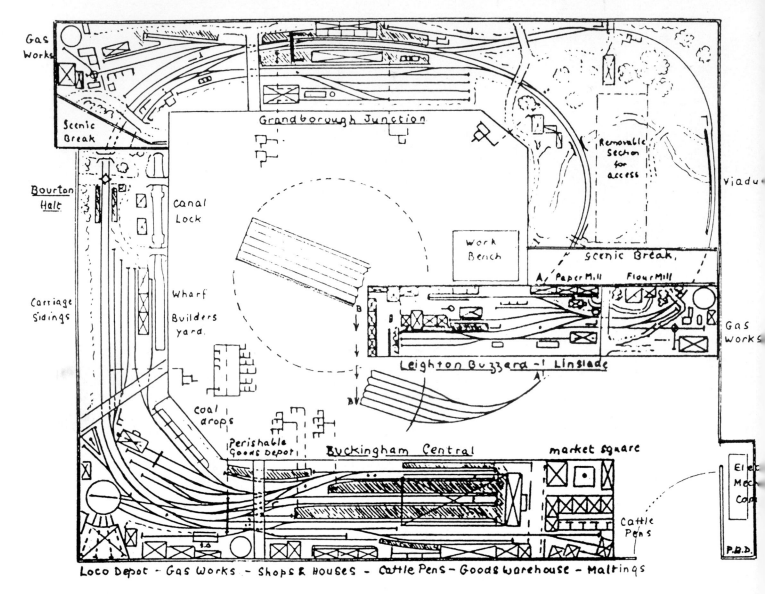

Gas Works

Scenic Break

Bourton Halt

Canal Lock

Carriage Sidings

Wharf

Builders yard

Grandborough Junction

Removable Section for access

Viadu

Work Bench

Scenic Break

A Paper Mill   Flour Mill

Gas Works

Coal drops

Leighton Buzzard - Linslade

Perishable Goods Depot

Buckingham Central   market square

Cattle Pens

Elec Mec Com

P.B.D.

Loco Depot - Gas Works - Shops & Houses - Cattle Pens - Goods Warehouse - Maltings

Cameo after cameo, vista after vista, I walked almost as in a dream, for my mind could not fully absorb the vast agglomeration of a lifetime's leisure work, and if I was in any doubt about the affection and respect in which this railway is held by most railway modellers – of any gauge – it was soon dispelled, for barely had I completed the programme, and even before it had been officially announced in the catalogue, bookings came pouring in for the loan of the programme, and have continued thus ever since.

When I thought we had covered just about every possible facet of Buckingham Central, Peter sprang another surprise on me. Explaining that his sons now having left home, he was often left on his own to operate the railway, so modern technology had been harnessed to his needs. He went to a cupboard near the doorway, opened it, and inside was a most astonishing assortment of wires, electrical gubbins, relays, a vast wheel mounted vertically with little arms reaching out over it in the manner of a musical-box, lights and all sorts of mysterious gadgetry.

"This" Peter explained "is my second operator when I am on my own." He went on to demonstrate the way this Heath-Robinson affair functioned by inviting me to offer a train from Grandborough Junction, and as I sent the bell-code signals, the computer answered, and when in due course the train was despatched, the computer took over. As if this were not enough, Peter demonstrated how, if he failed to despatch the train within reasonable time after offering it, the computer would nudge his memory with an angry burp, a red light would come on – and the railway clock would stop!

Track, scenery, buildings, lineside effects, locomotives, signals, wagons, coaches – all without exception the astonishing products of those skilful hands and innovative mind. At last I had seen it for myself.

Which reminds me – I MUST do something about putting up those kitchen shelves.

Opposite top – Grandborough Junction station and loco shed. The outside framed 4-4-0 heads a train of six wheeled carriages absorbed from the LD&ECR and still in their pre-1907 livery.

Opposite lower – A Marylebone express leaves Buckingham, passing the loco shed and goods sidings.   Photo – R. Prattley

James Kennedy
Gauge 1

"SO YOU ARE going to Scotland on holiday, are you?" said Ray Tustin as we sat in his living room after making a Guild programme on his 7mm model of Hampton Wick High Street. The year was 1981, and Arthur Dewar and I were planning a fortnight's holiday in the western Highlands and Islands. Ray continued – "Will you be going anywhere near Inverness? If so, you ought to try to visit James Kennedy's beautiful Gauge One Highland Railway there."

In fact we had planned a few days in Inverness at my favourite hotel on the bank of the River Ness, so I wrote to Mr. Kennedy asking if it would be convenient for us to visit him during our stay in Inverness, my letter bringing an immediate and cordial invitation to come and see him. He did add the proviso that any actual running of the trains would be dependent upon the weather – a stipulation with which I was all too familiar!

In due course we arrived in Inverness, but the day appointed for our visit turned out to be very wet indeed, so a phone call resulted in an alternative date being chosen, and that turned out to be a very pleasant late spring day. If the visit had been looked forward to by me, it was doubly so for Arthur Dewar, who himself models Highland Railway in 7mm scale, and Jim Kennedy had adopted the same period for his railway – the early 1900s.

Arriving at the house we were greeted by Jim and his wife, Jim reminding me of the popular image of a farmer. He was a big man who, before the 1939 war had been a livestock auctioneer, and when he joined the Army, they – with typical insistence on placing square pegs in round holes – sent him to the REME. It was whilst serving with this Regiment that Jim discovered within himself a natural aptitude for engineering, which explains the excellence of all his models, which were built to works drawings rather than model blueprints. Just how he came by these precious drawings is not clear, but living as he did in Inverness, he was conveniently close to the nerve-centre of the Highland Railway. He did show us some of these highly detailed drawings, but as even a simple blueprint can baffle me, they just filled me with wonder that they could be translated into the sleek models Jim produced.

He chose Gauge One as being the ideal medium for the garden railway, and also because it gave him room to fit the large motors,

which, incidentally, he insisted on being completely hidden from view. He went a step further by using fine standards for all his wheels, which he turned himself from castings, the wheel width being 5mm, the b-b 42mm, and the gauge 45mm. What was so astonishing was that in a garden which would have been none too large for Gauge 'O', his trains ran round curves of 8ft radius, these curves causing more problems than the 1 in 60 gradient between the two levels.

The garden, which was the fruits of over thirty years' development, was picturesque in the extreme, the paths, flora and general effects all being laid out with an artistic eye. The stations – two termini and two intermediate – were all of clearly recognisable Highland origin, while the signals of Holland and Mackenzie design were a highly attractive feature of the line. Those signals, however, were a source of heartbreaks to Jim, who, after spending heaven knows how many hours' labour, saw them reduced to matchwood in a matter of seconds. The cause of this was the school playground which lay high above the wall at the bottom of the garden, and, despite high wire-netting, allowed footballs to come over with devastating effect. All these signals had been brought out and placed in position for our benefit, one specially eye-catching – a beautiful multi-doll gantry guarding the entrance to one of the termini. "The school is on holiday now, so we are reasonably safe" he told us.

Some intuitively inspired urge had prompted me to bring plenty of film for my camera, and I started to take photographs from every possible angle. At the time there was no thought of making a Guild programme on this line, but in fact it was from these pictures, together with some lent to me by George Davidson, who had visited the line, which enabled George and me to cobble together a Guild audio-visual presentation on this remarkable railway.

"No-one in this town is interested" Jim told me "and I very seldom get even a second operator." Discussing this with George Davidson later, he pointed out that Jim was not Highland-born himself, but that the Kennedys came from Galloway and Ireland, probably coming here after the Clearances. Memories do not fade quickly in that part of the world! The fact remains that for much of the time Jim was driven back on his own resources.

It was quite clear that Jim derived most of his pleasure in the building of locomotives and rolling stock. He pointed out that the load-limit on a Highland 4-6-0 Castle climbing Struan bank was 205 tons; for a Loch or Ben 160 tons, so that his own Castle climbing his 1 in 60 bank with 10 coaches would be the equivalent of the prototype performance. His stud contact line delivered 24 volts, and an unusual feature of this was his practice of cross-bonding his running rails so as to give an improved path for the return current. Certainly while we were there the trains all ran faultlessly, despite the recent rain.

When we had spent an enjoyable hour or so on the railway we went indoors where Mrs Kennedy provided welcome refreshment, and we left the house with many vivid impressions of the railway and of a slightly sad feeling that more people did not share it with this hospitable man.

In 1984 Jim died, and his railway was in danger of being dispersed and virtually lost track of; indeed this did start to happen until Dr Tom Coombs of Nairn intervened. He made strenuous efforts to find homes for as many of the Kennedy locos and stock as possible – and with no little success. In fact, while I was staying with George Davidson in Scotland he produced two bulky packages which had just arrived, and which I helped him to unpack. In these were the Kennedy Barney 0-6-0 goods engine, a Cummings 4-4-0 No. 74 "DURN", plus one or two goods vehicles. It was also whilst staying with George that I first met Tom Coombs, although we had corresponded for some time. Tom Coombs' great ambition was to establish a working museum in or near Inverness – the cradle of the Highland Railway, where these magnificent models – or some of them, can run. Indeed, a site was found, in an abandoned school building at Fort George, but later, the building was requisitioned for other purposes, so it was back to square one. In a recent letter from Tom, he tells me that he is laying some Gauge One track in his own back garden alongside his Gauge 'O' system, so that James Kennedy's trains may once again be seen running in their native Scotland.

In conclusion I have to acknowledge the great help given to me by George Davidson and Tom Coombs whilst working on this chapter. It was by any standards a quite remarkable railway, and I think Jim would have been pleasantly surprised to know how inspirational it had proved.

Ron Andrews
Narrow Gauge

122

IT IS REMARKABLE how often I go to a house in order to make a programme on a model railway, only to find my attention going to things other than railways. So it was when I went to photograph Ron Andrews' garden railway on a beautiful early spring day, the garden a blaze of brilliant colour, and the house looking as if it has recently undergone a spring clean. I had not been there long before Ron spoke of Betty, who had sought out and planted the many shrubs and other flora which so enhanced the railway, making it all a very pleasant place. But he spoke of his wife in the past tense, and I soon learned that she died not long before. I never met her, but the state of the house and garden told me much about her, for her husband had seen to it

that it was all kept just as she would have cared for it herself; a remarkable tribute from a husband to his wife, (reminding me of another such example in Ian Machonachie, who was in a similar case).

Ron's railway was a narrow-gauge system running on Gauge 'O' track carrying vehicles and locomotives built to a scale of 12mm to the foot, and this gives me an opportunity to try to clarify some of the misconceptions caused by the confusion between the terms 'Gauge' and 'Scale'. We who model in Gauge 'O' do add to the confusion by calling our organisation "The Gauge 'O' Guild", for

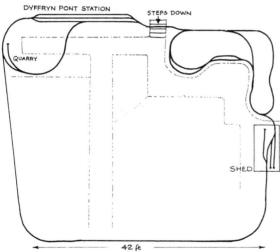

DYFFRYN PONT STATION   STEPS DOWN

QUARRY

SHED

← 42 ft →

the gauge refers merely to the distance between the rails. Models of a number of SCALES can run on Gauge 'O' track where the rails are roughly one and a quarter inches apart, making it possible to run 7mm, 10mm, 12mm, or even 16mm to the foot SCALE models on that track.

Ron has called his railway 'The Llynbach Scenic Railway' and it is not hard to infer from this that he has an affection for Welsh narrow-gauge lines – indeed, he and Betty enjoyed a holiday where their guest-house overlooked the Penrhyn quarry, with all its delightful little engines. The railway in Ron's garden deserves its name, for it is indeed scenic, with the track wending its tortuous way between miniature shrubs and trees. The garden slopes downwards fairly steeply from the house, so the section nearest the house is at ground level, while the railway runs at almost shoulder-height at the bottom of the garden.

The locomotives are all either scratch-built by Don, or adapted by him from commercial models, and a variety of motive power is to be found here, ranging from battery-control, live steam, or radio control over either of these methods.

At the bottom of the garden there is a shed through which the line runs, and this acts also as storage space for the trains when not in service. Stations, buildings, level crossings, and many lineside features are to be found on this railway, and at one point the line passes along the shore of a large lake where one can see a boat from which a man is fishing. A picturesque cottage stands nearby, while in another part of the garden there is a quarry with its low-level railway and workings. A hoist lifts the wagons from the floor of the quarry up to the high level transfer-sidings.

Before I left, Ron had another surprise in store for me, for we made our way to his garage where he housed a pre-war Austin 'Ascot' saloon – the exact replica of one I drove in 1938. Some time after my visit to photograph Lynbach, I met Ron at a model railway exhibition and found that he had driven there in that beautifully restored Austin, now in truly immaculate condition. He handed me the ignition key, inviting me to take the car for a run. I needed no second bidding and very soon realised just what a succession of cars since the war had done to me, for I had almost forgotten how to double-declutch, forgotten what non-synchro-mesh gears were like, and just how heavy that steering was. However, in five minutes I had turned back the calendar over half a century and was back in my old car again. Fifteen minutes of pure nostalgia, and in the deserted country lanes which surrounded us I was convinced that the horror of motorways had never really happened, and that if I drove to Ipswich station I would see emerging from the tunnel a shining green B12 4-6-0 with a train of bow-ended Gresley teak stock.

Nigel Goff

Narrow Gauge

T HE FASCINATION of a model railway is always greatly enhanced when it is based on a known locale, and there must be many people who have visited the Island of Skye. Nigel Goff has built his narrow gauge light railway over a route which was in fact mooted at one time, but never actually materialised. One has only to see the terrain to appreciate the formidable obstacles of civil engineering which confronted anyone who wanted to build a railway on the island.

Skye always reminds me of a cushion which has been squeezed in the middle, causing two very uneven bulges, one on the north and the other south, with the narrow waist boasting a solitary, but impressive Sligachan hotel. On the north-east coast stands the only town on the island, Portree, the 'ree' stemming from 'regal' or 'rex', for the port was used by King James. On the opposite side of that northern bulge of the 'squashed cushion' is the village of Dunvegan, with its castle, the traditional seat of the MacLeods.

Most visitors to the island will land at Kyleakin, having taken the ferry over the narrow Kyle of Lochalsh, reaching that incredibly beautiful spot either by train from Inverness, or by road. The southern bulge in the cushion, containing Armadale (for Mallaig) does not concern us here, for the railway disdains this half of the island.

Nigel's railway starts at Kyleakin – often mispronounced as 'Kyle-eekin' – and makes its unlikely way to Portree. From there the railway turns due east and crosses the island to Dunvegan, which is the terminus. Had that railway ever been built it would have passed through some spectacular scenery – which would include the backdrop of the dominating feature of Skye – the Cuillin Mountain range, with White Cuillins (which are actually pink!) and the gaunt Black Cuillins. The whole area is known locally as 'The Cuillin'.

'J.B. Earle', a 2-6-4 tank locomotive from the Leek & Manifold.

Right – a diesel locomotive runs around the stock of the 'Hebridean Express' formed of ex Leek & Manifold stock.

Once again we find ourselves up against the often confused business of scale and gauge. The track here is 'O' Gauge but the trains are built principally to a scale of ½" to the foot. There are a few models of smaller scale, but all run on Gauge 'O' track.

It is easy to see that by realising in model form what was only proposed in fact, Nigel has given free rein to his interest in narrow gauge railways, for here you will see vehicles from the Welshpool and Llanfair Railway, the Leek and Manifold, and even the Campbeltown and Machrihanish Light Railway. In fact, included in the goods stock are examples of coal wagons built by Nigel Macmillan, whose smaller scale model of the Campbeltown and Machrihanish Light Railway appears in another chapter.

There are many advantages in working to this particular scale, for the size of the locomotives provides plenty of room to use quite substantial motors even in very low-boilered engines. One feature of the loco stud which caught my eye was the use of articulated locomotives, built on a similar principle to the well-known double Fairlie engines of the Ffestiniog Railway in Wales.

The couplings are of the Norwegian (central) single coupling type where a hook engages in a slot in the opposing buffer-head, but, as Nigel explained to me, these couplings were extremely prone to coming apart, so two chains were fitted to the headstocks and provided a safety measure should a coupling fail. These chains are also modelled on Nigel's engines.

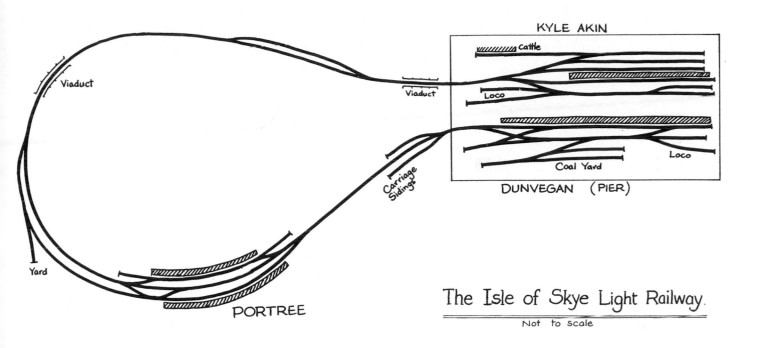

KYLE AKIN

Cattle

Loco

Coal Yard

Loco

DUNVEGAN (PIER)

Viaduct

Viaduct

Carriage Sidings

Yard

PORTREE

The Isle of Skye Light Railway.

Not to scale

'Norbury' rests at Dunvegan where a new loco shed is under construction.

A skilled craftsman in the use of styrene, many of the engines and rolling stock are built from this material, and it is difficult to see that they are not of metal construction. He takes this a step further; one of the viaducts between Kyleakin and Sligachan is built from expanded polystyrene, taken from the packing material used to send so many electrical items these days. These he forms into the required shapes and then with a length of copper wire fixed to soldering iron he 'burns' the brickwork or stonework into the material before painting it with suitable colours. The amazing thing is that the viaduct had – at the time of writing – been out in all weathers for over twelve years.

I was surprised to see a smart coach painted in GWR chocolate and cream running on this line, and asked Nigel how that came to be there. He explained that the vehicle had been acquired by the Isle of Skye Light Railway Company from the Welshpool and Llanfair line which was taken over in its final years by the Great Western Railway.

The pride of the line is the Hebridean Boat Train, comprising two beautiful yellow coaches and suitable locomotive, and running between Dunvegan and Kyleakin. These coaches have verandah ends with the most intricate filigree ironwork in the verandah rails, which, so Nigel says, was not too difficult to make.

"But" he added "a trifle tedious perhaps."

MODEL
RAILWAYS
AND THEIR
BUILDERS

148

Phil Crathorn

Narrow Gauge

S SO OFTEN HAPPENS, I first heard of Phil Crathorn through the pages of a model railway magazine, where Tony Wright's superb photographs immediately captured my imagination. The article described an exhibition layout in 7mm scale – although, being narrow-gauge, the track was closer to 00 scale than 0. Through the courtesy of the magazine editor, David Brown, I was able to to contact Phil, seeking his permission to make a Guild programme on this fine representation of part of the erstwhile Lynton and Barnstaple Railway. The model is known as 'LYNTON & LYNMOUTH' and is one of those comparatively rare examples of a specific area and period being represented.

Phil and his wife, Margaret, made me extremely welcome when in due course I presented myself at their house, where I discovered that Phil was a civil engineer, this doubtless playing an important part in his research into his chosen locale, which proved to be the last mile or so of the old Lynton & Barnstaple Railway before it ran into Lynton and Lynmouth station. With so many holiday-makers

visiting this beautiful spot, it will be generally known that Lynmouth lies on the north Devon coast where the Lyn river flows into the Atlantic. The river was the scene of the most terrible devastation and loss of life some years ago when a series of concurrent freak events caused sudden flooding, almost within a matter of minutes.

The narrow-gauge railway ran from Barnstaple, an important town on the River Taw, through the picturesque Devonshire countryside, and climbing from the Taw valley until it ended high above the little port of Lynmouth. Phil has chosen to model the terminus in its original form, although it was in fact extended in 1926 when the Southern Railway took the line over. The entire station, with its bay platform, main platform, run-round loop, and goods depot is accurately modelled and fully signalled, and is operated exactly as was the prototype in its heyday, when, during the holiday season, the line would carry many thousands of visitors. Trains were almost invariably of mixed passenger and goods stock, with 1st and 3rd class accommodation for passengers. Phil has built almost everything on this railway himself, including three Manning Wardle locomotives named YEO, TAW and LEW, plus a delightful Baldwin engine named LYN.

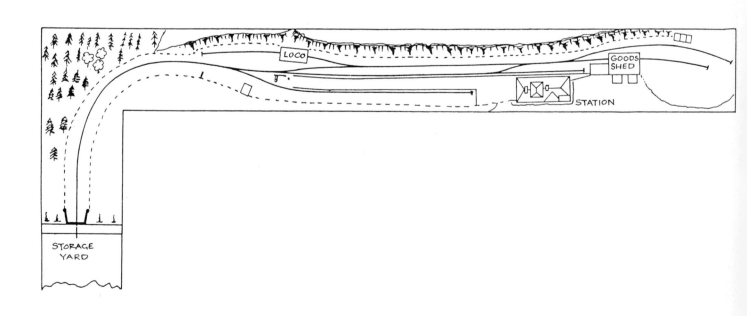

When not on exhibition, the railway is housed in a shed in the very attractive garden behind the house, with the fiddle-yard spanning the doorway. The layout is in the shape of a shallow L, the fiddle-yard and Caffins Halt bridge on the shorter leg. Emerging from hidden sidings from under a road overbridge, the single track line passes heavily wooded country in the area of Barbrook Woods – well known to walkers in the area.

Whereas many of the people whose railways I photograph are old friends, and therefore well-known to me, there are others, such as Phil Crathorn, whom I have met only once, and it would be presumptuous of me to essay a character-study on so short an acquaintance. However, one cannot help but retain some impressions of the people encountered in this nationwide search for notable model railways, and my memory is of a beautifully kept home in a very pleasant suburb of a Midlands town, where these two hospitable people live a very civilised life-style. This impression was enhanced when the discreet hi-fi was switched on – not to the sort of thing we are subjected to almost wherever we go these days – the interminable stream of pop, but Lalo's Symphonie Espagnole. In fact, I used that music as the introductory and closing music for the Guild audio-visual programme on LYNTON & LYNMOUTH.

MODEL
RAILWAYS
AND THEIR
BUILDERS

George Barlow

15″ Gauge

THERE ARE THOSE who will take issue with me when I include the Romney, Hythe & Dymchurch Railway in Kent, in a book on model railways, for, they will argue, that is a miniature railway – not a model railway. Well, I am sorry gentlemen, but whilst admitting that it has become customary to differentiate between the smaller gauges and the larger, passenger railways by these distinctions, I seek refuge in my dictionary, which defines a model as '– an exact three-dimensional representation of an object, in miniature.'

It is impossible to speak of the RH&DR without mentioning the name of George Barlow, for he is probably the only surviving member of that railway who worked with and for Captain Howey, the man mainly responsible for the creation of the railway. I have known George for some 20 years now, and during that time we have become very good friends, with our birthdays a matter of only weeks apart in 1916. He never allows me to forget that he is my senior!

I doubt if there are many men who have been included in the Birthday Honours by reason of their services to miniature railways, but this happened to George when he retired officially from the RH&D Railway. He has been involved in many historic occasions in the history of the line, and perhaps none gave him more pleasure than the running of a special train in 1986, on his seventieth birthday, with a headboard inscribed "THE GEORGIAN". He tells me that this headboard is to be brought out again for a special train in 1996 on his eightieth birthday.

His natural talent for public speaking, his warm personality and articulate, unhesitant delivery have brought him invitations to lecture in many parts of the world, including the USA and Australia. During the early 1990s he suffered a serious heart operation which went wrong, and he spent nearly a month in intensive care; in fact, the computer dictated that his life-support machine should be switched off as he had barely a shadow of a chance of recovery. Computers obviously don't know George, for more than two years later he is leading a very active life, which includes driving his 2½″ gauge TUGBOAT ANNIE, built by LBSC in 1942, on the Romney Marsh Model Engineering Society's track.

It was 1946 when young George was demobbed from the Royal Engineers, where he had been a locomotive driver, and at the age of 30 realised that he was too old to apply for a driving job on the railways. It was then that he spotted an advertisement in the Model Engineer, asking for a driver on a miniature railway, so he wrote, applying for an interview. From that date to this, he heard nothing, but he did wonder if the advert emanated from the RH&DR, so he wrote to them, asking if this was so. He received a reply in which they denied being the author of that advert, but that in fact they were looking for a driver for that year. So began a fifty-year long close association with the 15″ railway which runs from Hythe, southwards to Dungeness.

Captain Howey's partner in the early days of the railway was killed at Monza in his racing car, leaving Howey alone to direct the fortunes of the line. He was not always an easy man to get on with, and one of his pet aversions was having his photograph taken, yet such was George Barlow's persuasive powers that he was able to furnish me with several photos. Howey also took a dislike to the two American type engines, and after one trip, refused to drive them any more.

Although George has always regarded GREEN GODDESS as his own special charge, he drove all the engines at times. Curiously enough, although I have travelled behind the GODDESS several times, when it came to a footplate trip it was on DR. SYN, with George in charge. In 1925 GREEN GODDESS underwent her trials on the Ravenglass and Eskdale Railway in Cumbria, and not long ago George was able to drive that engine once again over that picturesque line – a vastly different locale from the flat marshland of Kent. With severe gradients and curves, the Ratty has to be 'driven' every inch of the way.

In the early 'seventies, after Captain Howey's death, the railway all but closed, for local conditions were rapidly changing. No longer were the hotels thronged with holiday-makers who would spend their annual fortnight's holiday in Folkestone, Hythe, or Romney; no more were the holiday camps packed with young people, and no more did these visitors spend much time travelling on the little railway. They were partly replaced with day-trippers who came in the family car, and the fortunes of the railway were in a desperate condition. It was at this time that Sir William McAlpine came to the rescue (not the first instance of this generous man saving some precious part of our railway history!), and under the aegis of John Snell's able management, the railway has survived until today. If those who spend vast sums of money on film and video tape would divert some of that cash into travelling on the railway instead of merely photographing it from the lineside, the management would breathe far more easily. The

GREEN GODDESS undergoing running trials on the Raven-glass & Eskdale Railway. Henry Greenly stands in shirtsleeves in the background. The photograph was taken at Dalegarth in June 1925 and the locomotives modelled on Gresley's A1 Pacifics which first appeared just three years previously.

George Barlow collection

railway's contract to convey children to and from school at New Romney throughout the year has helped to stabilise the situation, but it is a sad fact of life that the thousands of lineside photographers seem to think that by photographing the railway they have made adequate contribution to its survival. So far as I am aware, the Romney, Hythe, and Dymchurch Railway are not major shareholders in Kodak.

The railway is a living, working memorial not only to Captain Howey, but to the man who designed all the engines, the loco sheds, and stations, Henry Greenly. Greenly was therefore not very pleased when in 1926 the then Duke of York (later King George VI) visited the railway and Howey neglected to introduce him to the Duke. It was an unforgivable slight which Greenly never forgot.

Retirement has given him time to develop his other interests, including model railways, and he now possesses many HO scale models and a growing collection of 7mm scale engines. No longer is George Barlow to be seen on the footplate of his beloved GREEN GODDESS in its immaculate green livery with its

Captain Howey 1962.   *George Barlow collection*

GREEN GODDESS at Hythe, 1973. George Barlow stands in the turntable well while preparing the locomotive for the days duties.

shining brass pipework – always kept polished no matter what the weather – nor is the familiar figure to be seen, long after the railway has closed to the public in the evenings, working in the shed, cleaning out the tubes and going over every inch of the engine he knows and loves so well before he thinks of making his way home – perhaps to share a pint with me before going to his evening meal. But like a benevolent guardian angel his spirit survives on the railway, and his influence will long survive his daily attendance there.

It is conjectural whether he (or I for that matter) will see the GEORGIAN run on his hundredth birthday, for it is highly likely that by then, Guy's Hospital will have evolved a more ruthless computer.

Epilogue

AS I WRITE the final pages to this book I am only too aware of its shortcomings and – more importantly – its omissions. As long as I am able I shall continue in my search for fresh fields and pastures new.

The fifteen years of my retirement have been a sort of dream – a new life – where I have been privileged to visit and photograph scores of model railways, many of which I would never have heard of had it not been for the scheme I started in 1980, nor, I strongly suspect, would anyone else other than those closely concerned, have heard of them.

I have prepared the grist, and now it has gone to the mill of my publishers, firstly David Jenkinson, and latterly David Joy, with both of whom it has been a pleasure to work. Fine millers, these two, as is my good friend, Barry Lane, who designed the book.

The germ of the idea for the book came from James Opie of the Railway Book Club; look what you have done, James!

The dedication is to the Gauge 'O' Guild who have so whole-heartedly supported me in all my efforts, but whatever merit this volume may have lies principally in the friendly co-operation of the modellers themselves. To them the glory!

Don Neale's magnificent 7mm 'Trafalgar' . . . see page 37.